SpringerBriefs in Economics

SpringerBriefs present concise summaries of cutting-edge research and practical applications across a wide spectrum of fields. Featuring compact volumes of 50 to 125 pages, the series covers a range of content from professional to academic. Typical topics might include:

- A timely report of state-of-the art analytical techniques
- A bridge between new research results, as published in journal articles, and a contextual literature review
- A snapshot of a hot or emerging topic
- An in-depth case study or clinical example
- A presentation of core concepts that students must understand in order to make independent contributions

SpringerBriefs in Economics showcase emerging theory, empirical research, and practical application in microeconomics, macroeconomics, economic policy, public finance, econometrics, regional science, and related fields, from a global author community.

Briefs are characterized by fast, global electronic dissemination, standard publishing contracts, standardized manuscript preparation and formatting guidelines, and expedited production schedules.

Ednaldo Araquém Silva

U.S. Corporate Profits, 1950–2024

Operating Profit Markups in Leading U.S. Firms

Springer

Ednaldo Araquém Silva
EdgarStat®
Chevy Chase, MD, USA

ISSN 2191-5504 ISSN 2191-5512 (electronic)
SpringerBriefs in Economics
ISBN 978-3-032-11398-6 ISBN 978-3-032-11399-3 (eBook)
https://doi.org/10.1007/978-3-032-11399-3

This Springer imprint is published by the registered company Springer Nature Switzerland AG
The registered company address is: Gewerbestrasse 11, 6330 Cham, Switzerland

Acronyms and Data Source

REVT refers to operating revenue derived from the net sales (after returns and allowances) of goods or services.

COGS refers to the cost of goods sold or the direct costs of production, including materials, direct labor, and inventory adjustments. In Standard & Poor's Compustat (my primary data source), COGS includes certain impairment charges.

XSGA refers to operating expenses not directly linked to specific products or services; also known as Selling, General, and Administrative Expenses.

XOPR (Total Cost) is the sum of COGS and XSGA.

OIBDP is operating income or profit before depreciation, depletion, and amortization.

Data Source: REVT, COGS, XSGA, and XOPR were obtained from *Compustat* (standardized data); figures from other vendors (e.g., Mergent, Compact Disclosure) cannot be mixed without disclosed prior reconciliation.

The amounts of REVT and XOPR are reported in millions of United States dollars (USD).

Acknowledgments

To my mentors, Chad Claussen and Alain de Janvry; to my family, Miriam Silva, Rita Gama, Laura Craveiro, and Luisa Silva; and my coworkers, Julia Vasconcellos, Bartosz Niejadlik, Joanna Jeziorek, and Joshua Jones.

I thank academics Jon Breslaw and Allin Cottrell for their review of my book. They urged a broader literature survey, but I found no published studies that use the same dependent variable; studies with other profit measures are not comparable.

Competing Interests The author has no competing interests to declare that are relevant to the content of this manuscript.

Contents

About the Author

Ednaldo Araquém Silva, Ph.D. (University of California, Berkeley), is an economist and founder of EdgarStat LLC, whose work applies corporate-level financial data and econometrics to the study of profitability and intergroup transfer-pricing. He served as a senior economic adviser at the IRS Office of Chief Counsel, was a Senior Vice President at Wyeth Pharmaceuticals, and taught graduate economics at The New School.

Introduction

U.S. corporations' operating profits are not well-researched. I address this gap by analyzing the markup of operating profits (before depreciation, depletion, and amortization) for U.S. corporations across 11 industries: petroleum and natural gas exploration, beverages, manufacturing, pharmaceutical preparations, chemicals and allied products, petroleum refining, machinery and equipment, computer equipment and electronic devices, transportation equipment, government contractors, and computer services.[1]

Three to eight corporations are represented in each industry. This choice highlights the most prominent corporations in every sector, many appearing in rankings like the S&P 500 and Fortune 500 over the years.[2]

I use corporation-level data from 1950 to 2024 to analyze the behavior of operating profits (OIBDP or EBITDA) before discretionary deductions, such as depreciation, depletion, and amortization, by examining the relationship between revenue and total costs, which encompass the composite accounts of COGS (Cost of Goods Sold) and XSGA (operating expenses), referred to as XOPR.[3]

The primary finding of this study is that the operating profit markup, which refers to the slope coefficient of the regression equation between REVT (net sales) and XOPR (total cost), is linear and shows no changes, breaks, or switch points in slope over the long-term period examined. The operating profit markup before depreciation and amortization for each examined corporation is high (there are a few noted exceptions); although values may vary across certain industries, the long-run stability of the operating profit markup is visible.

[1] To the extent that impairments are included in COGS, operating profits as used in this book are understated.

[2] Chandler (1962) recounts the rise of oligopoly in the U.S. economy and includes several case studies (DuPont, GM, Standard Oil (New Jersey, later renamed Exxon, now ExxonMobil, and Sears, Roebuck).

[3] COGS differs from the abstract economics concept of variable cost. In addition to the purchase of materials (raw, semi-finished, and finished goods) and direct labor, COGS includes one-period change in inventories and other unstructured cost schedules.

The five exceptions to the estimated high long-run operating profit markups per corporation are Ashland (GVKEY 001794) 3%, Celanese (162254) 2%, Goodyear Tire (005234) 2%, Occidental Petroleum (008068) negative, and Valero Energy (015247) 4.8%. The nominal (not PPI adjusted) operating profit markup of Occidental Petroleum is 35.5%. See Exhibit 2.

The starting year since 1950 is contingent upon the availability of the annual coordinated pairs XOPR and REVT data for the corporations being examined. Exhibit 1 provides the number of corporations per industry.

To the best of my knowledge, no published study uses U.S. corporation-level OIBDP as the dependent variable. The works surveyed use other measures; most use net profit, which includes passive income and depreciation, depletion, amortization, and interest deductions. This usual measure is less reliable because it mixes operating and non-operating corporate activities.

For example, Dennis Mueller's corporation-level research was published in 1986 and covered 600 U.S. corporations from 1950 to 1972. The work, *Profits in the Long Run*, was published by Cambridge University Press in 1986. Mueller's first-degree recursive econometric model (AR(1)) was later expanded to include several countries, such as Canada, England, France, Germany, and Japan, as part of a joint research project. This project was published in the volume edited by Dennis Mueller, *The Dynamics of Company Profits: An International Comparison*, Cambridge University Press, 1990.

Muller's U.S. data coverage was updated from 1972 to 1999 and a higher order autoregressive mechanism was examined by Adelina Gschwandtner (2012).[4] This prior research considers a different dependent variable (net profit instead of operating profits divided by total assets) from my research and aggregates corporate accounting data into groups while I examine individual corporations. The two research projects are not comparable because the dependent variables are different.

Exhibit 1

Industry	SIC code(s)	Corporations count
Petroleum and Natural Gas	1311	5
Beverages	2080; 2085; 2086	3
Manufacturing	2670; 2834; 2860; 3011	6
Pharmaceutical	2834	7
Chemicals and Allied Products	2810; 2820; 2834; 2851; 2860; 2870	7
Petroleum Refining	2911	7
Machinery and Equipment	3510; 3523; 3531; 3679	4
Computer Equipment and Electronic Devices	3559; 3570; 3576; 3663; 3674	8
Transportation Equipment	3711; 3714; 3728; 3760; 9997	8
Government Contractors	3721; 3724; 3760; 3812	8
Computer Services	5961; 7370; 7372; 7373	8
	Total number of corporations	*71*

[4] Gschwandtner posits the untested hypothesis that the net profit over total assets of the sampled U.S. corporations decreased during the period covered from 1950 to 1999 because of international competition.

Chapter 1
Cost-Based Profits

I analyze the econometric relationship between revenue and total costs for major US corporations. I conduct a regression analysis of 71 companies, using a reduced-form equation to determine the operating profit markup for each sampled company. There is a simple arithmetic relationship between the profit markup and the profit margin.[1]

I distinguish between accounting and structural equations, also known as behavioral equations. Structural equations can be specified in several algebraic functional forms, such as linear or log-linear (power function), and are subject to random errors.[2]

Several estimation techniques are available to address the misbehavior of the regression residual errors—I adopted the Newey-West heteroskedasticity and

[1] The operating profit markup is based on total cost (XOPR), and the profit margin is based on revenue (REVT). As ratios, the numerator is the same, but the denominators are different.

[2] Rather than presupposing a linear or log-linear form, I start by exploratory data analysis (EDA). First, I inspect the XOPR vs. REVT scatterplots to see the functional shape and any leverage points. Second, I scout the scatterplots using Loess, which is a nonparametric local regression curve fitting algorithm. Third, I then fit the least-squares curve and estimate the **intercept** and **slope (markup)** coefficients, using residual plots and fit diagnostics to confirm that the selected curve fit is adequate; transformations are used only if the data warrant them. The assignment of dependent and independent variables follows the economics: operating costs (XOPR) drive revenue (REVT) through price pass-through, not the reverse. This cost-based theory of prices is known since the classical economists, including Adam Smith, David Ricardo, and Karl Marx.

E. A. Silva, *U.S. Corporate Profits, 1950–2024*, SpringerBriefs in Economics,
https://doi.org/10.1007/978-3-032-11399-3_1

autocorrelation consistent (HAC) standard errors.[3] I do not estimate structural equations because they may omit relevant variables, which can lead to biased estimates.[4]

The econometric analysis begins with the ordered pairs of total cost (excluding depreciation, depletion, and amortization) versus operating revenue, which I illustrate using scatterplots. As stated, the individual corporate regression spans the period from 1950 to 2024, depending on the availability of data from individual companies (see the exhibits at the end of each chapter).

A simple linear equation fits the historical corporate data very well, except for Occidental Petroleum, whose data are better represented by a power function. The initial linear regression equation fitted per individual corporation in the sample is:

$$\text{REVT} = \lambda_0 + \lambda_1 \, \text{XOPR} \tag{1.1}$$

where REVT denotes operating revenue (net sales) and XOPR denotes total costs and expenses.[5]

The derivation of the estimated regression equation is presented in Appendix 1. The power function is estimated by taking the natural logarithms of the dependent and independent variables.

The guideline for assessing the significance of coefficients is that the *t*-statistic exceeds the critical value of 1.96; however, lower values may also be considered significant.[6]

To test the effect of producer price inflation (PPI, Index 1982 = 100), I tested an expanded (PPI adjustment) model:

[3] The HAC algorithm is used to recalculate the variance-covariance matrix of the ordinary least-squares (OLS) coefficients, so the *t*-statistics and confidence intervals remain valid even when residuals are (a) uneven in size across observations (heteroskedastic) and/or (b) correlated over time (autocorrelated). HAC does not change the regression coefficients or R^2. HAC changes the standard errors: typically, larger if the residuals are serially correlated or heteroskedastic.

[4] Several econometric textbooks elaborate the distinction between accounting and structural equations, and the conceptual error estimating structural equations, my favorite is Jan Kmenta, *Elements of Econometrics* (2nd edition) Macmillan, 1986, section 10–4 (Specification Errors).

[5] In Standard & Poor's Compustat database nomenclature, REVT is operating revenue (excluding passive income, such as interest, dividends, rents, royalties, or capital gains), and XOPR is total operating expenses (COGS + XSGA), excluding DP (depreciation, amortization, and depletion).

[6] The *t*-statistic is a measure of reliability and is computed as the ratio of the estimated coefficient to its standard error. Thus, the higher the *t*-statistic, the more reliable is the estimated coefficient. The $t > 1.96$ value is a convention and not an undisputed number.

$$\mathrm{REVT} = \lambda_0 + \lambda_1\,\mathrm{XOPR} + \lambda_2\,\mathrm{PPI} \tag{1.2}$$

Regression model (1.2), applied at the individual US corporation level and covering the full 1950–2024 period, appears novel in the published literature I can find. An expected alternative of deflating REVT by an *output price index* and XOPR by an *input price index* is not viable for the extended period covered in this book because no consistent series of such deflators exists. I discuss this unviable choice of deflators below.

More elaborate econometric specifications are possible—for example, rewriting (1.2) as a structural ECM/ARDL model, or "double-deflating," by applying separate output and input producer-price indices (deflating REVT by an output PPI and XOPR by an input PPI).

In practice, both paths add complexity with limited benefit. ECM/ARDL requires lag selection, cointegration tests, and extra parameters that cost degrees of freedom (not a measure problem given my long time series) and distract from the main message: cross-corporations and industry differences alongside a stable long-run operating-profit markup and clear pass-through of input-price changes at the corporation (not grouped or aggregated) level.

Moreover, output/input deflators tailored to each corporation are not available for multiproduct, multi-business segment companies; using multiple PPIs invites measurement error and undermines comparability. For these reasons, I keep the simpler specification in regression Eq. (1.2): transparent, replicable among individual corporations and across industries, and sufficient to document stable markups and pass-through input total cost changes.

Since the variables XOPR and REVT in my work are nominal, PPI measures the economy-wide producer price-level shocks and is a substitute specification to deflating (inflation adjusting) the dependent and independent variables.

The partial regression coefficient on XOPR captures the corporation-level link between operating costs and revenue. In the hypothetical "firm" of microeconomics textbooks in which each entity or corporation produces or sells a single product or service, expression (1.1) is the price equation marked up on total average costs (excluding depreciation and other discretionary noncash or accrual charges such as amortization, depletion, or impairment not included in COGS).[7]

The partial regression coefficient on the variable PPI measures how much industry-wide producer prices shift a corporation's revenue holding nominal costs fixed. The PPI variable has the effect of isolating the pricing power (or the ability to

[7] My Eq. (1.1) better reflects the individual corporation's practice of maintaining a fixed **operating-profit** markup over total operating costs and expenses (XOPR). By contrast, Kalecki's pricing rule sets price as a markup over "unit prime cost"—materials plus direct wages—that is, COGS and not over total operating costs (COGS + XSGA). Kalecki's (1965) equations (1) and (2) imply a degree-of-oligopoly markup on prime costs; overheads affect the markup only indirectly. Hence my price Eq. (1.1) differs substantively in what cost base the price is being marked up.

pass through total cost increases to customers) of individual corporations. Since the coefficients of PPI are not relevant for demonstrating my theses, I leave this book uncluttered with irrelevant information.

The statistical tables reflect the partial regression coefficient of XOPR from model (1.2). Appendix 2 features a PPI (all commodities) chart from 1950 through 2024. Model (1.2) is reported with the Newey-West corrected standard errors.[8]

The PPI coefficient was significant in 34 observations of the 71 companies.[9] The industry most affected by PPI is the petroleum exploration and production (Chap. 3), in which the PPI coefficient was significant for all five tested corporations.[10] The downstream petroleum refining industry (Chap. 8) revealed the opposite, with the PPI coefficients being insignificant for six of the seven tested corporations.

In the beverage industry (Chap. 4), all three tested corporations show insignificant PPI coefficients. Across the remaining industries covered in this book, the significance of the PPI coefficient was mixed, with 27 corporations showing a significant coefficient and 28 showing an insignificant coefficient.

[8] As stated before, meriting repetition: Newey-West (HAC) standard errors adjust the standard errors of the regression coefficients—not the coefficients—so the *t*-statistics and confidence intervals stay reliable when regression residuals are (a heteroskedastic (error size varies across observations) and/or (b) autocorrelated (errors are correlated across nearby periods). See https://www.jstatsoft.org/article/download/v011i10/19

[9] There are 71 companies in the sample. Marathon Oil is divided into two periods because of a gap in reported data. The two observation periods report different coefficients for XOPR and a different significance in the PPI coefficient (the 1950–1981 period does not have a significant PPI coefficient, while the 1988–2024 period has a significant PPI coefficient).

[10] Chapter 3 includes five corporations but six company observations due to the two distinct periods of Marathon Oil arising from a gap in reported data. The 1950–1981 period does not have a significant PPI coefficient, while the 1988–2024 period has a significant PPI coefficient.

Chapter 2
Time-Invariant Markup

This chapter follows the classical economic framework, highlighting the causal relationship between a company's cost structure and operating profits. Kalecki (1965, Ch. 1, "Cost and Prices") is my principal theoretical inspiration. From this perspective, revenue (REVT) and operating profits (OIBDP), often referred to as the "profits of enterprise," are fundamentally influenced by XOPR.

I am unable to find prior research related to my work because the choice of dependent variable in prior research is different and the level of data aggregation is also different. Dennis Mueller's research (1986, 1990), as the closest example, who prompted several follow-ups, introduced an autoregressive approach to modeling corporate profitability over time. His first-order difference equations provided a framework that lacked a structural economic foundation. The first-order autoregressive (AR(1)) model reduces to a weighted sum of random shocks, offering little insight into the underlying cost-driven mechanisms of profit formation. Mueller's followers, model and data extenders, have not departed from the autoregressive mechanism, extending from AR(1) to AR(4), for example, but excluding structural variables from the empirical approach. See Gschwandtner (2012), Eq. (7) and Table 1, which has a survey of prior published research under Mueller's and related research program. Her Table A2 contains the results of estimating from AR(1) to AR(4) autoregressive mechanisms, unperturbed by the principle of parsimony or Occam's razor.[1]

[1] Gschwandtner's (2012) Table 6 has the regression results of certain structural characteristics for her six groups of corporations. The characteristics include concentration measures, industry size, industry growth, market share, individual corporation growth (aggregated), and corporate size (measured by the log of total assets). Several of these variables are colinear, and thus the partial regression coefficients are unreliable. This structural component shows the mixed origins of Gschwandtner's research, inheriting the AR model from Mueller and the structural model from Bain (1956). This flexible approach can be confusing, more like a survey of published research on aggregate ROA (again not the topic of my book on US corporate operating profit markup (flow variable, dimensionless concept) based in disaggregated financials).

E. A. Silva, *U.S. Corporate Profits, 1950–2024*, SpringerBriefs in Economics,
https://doi.org/10.1007/978-3-032-11399-3_2

Gschwandtner extends Mueller's original US corporation sample period from 1972 to 1999, breaking the period into three subperiods from 1950 to 1966, 1967 to 1983, and 1984 to 1999. The period breaks are heuristic, not determined by statistical measures. Like Mueller and his other research cohorts, Gschwandtner aggregates the large sample of individual corporations into several groups, whose composition is arbitrary. Thus, Mueller and his cohort's research program differs from my research presented here in several important respects.

First, I analyze individual corporations and fit individual regressions (model 1.2) instead of fitting group regressions. My work is as disaggregated as the data allows. Second, I use a structural model (containing XOPR as the explanatory variable) that is not reduced by recursive substitutions (like theirs) to a sum of random events. Third, I examine operating profits before depreciation, depletion, and amortization (OIADP or EBITDA), and they examine net profits divided by total assets.[2]

In Mueller and Gschwandtner, the dependent variable is return on assets (ROA)—net profits divided by (typically average) total assets. ROA mixes operating and nonoperating components: net income aggregates core operating accounts with items such as interest income/expense, dividends, realized gains/losses, rents, royalties, and fair-value adjustments—flows that can be independent of the corporation's primary business.

The denominator, total assets, also embeds acquisition accounting (goodwill and other acquired identifiable intangibles, subject to amortization or impairment) and grows with financing-driven expansions (e.g., debt-funded acquisitions), even though leverage itself sits on the liability side. Consequently, net income is sensitive to judgment heavy, often noncash charges (e.g., goodwill impairment) that may be weakly tied to current operating activity. For measuring operating markups and price pass-through, ROA is therefore a noisy and less comparable proxy than an operating profit-based measure. To this problem, consider that ROA is not a dimensionless variable, dependent on the acquisition cost recognition and the assigned longevity to the long-lasting assets on the corporation's balance sheet.

Another difference is that I measure level variables, XOPR and REVT, and the referenced research, including the work of Stigler (1963), measures ratio variables. My research uses absolute categories, which are more sensible when taking one-period differences, and they use ratio categories.

---

[2]It is not possible to purge **impairment** effects from the historical XOPR series. In Compustat, some impairment charges are **embedded** in COGS (e.g., inventory write-downs), and others appear in **XSGA** or as separate "special items"; coverage of dedicated impairment fields is incomplete and inconsistent over time. As a result, **XOPR ≡ COGS + XSGA** can include judgment-driven impairments that are not reliably identifiable. Consequently, **operating profit before depreciation, depletion, and amortization (OIBDP = REVT − XOPR)** may be **understated** in years with such charges.

2.1 Classical Cost Structure and its Challenges

Classical economists break down total costs into direct and indirect labor expenditures. However, this analytical distinction proves challenging to apply across a diverse dataset of US corporations spanning over seven decades.[3] Aggregated financial reporting removes the details needed to classify expenses by labor type, and the evolution of corporate operations adds complexities that resist any rigid categorization.[4]

Thus, a viable approach is empirical and data driven, emphasizing total operating expenditures (denoted XOPR = COGS + XSGA) as the determinant of revenue REVT.[5] Rather than segmenting costs, the model captures the relationship between revenues and a consolidated cost metric at the company level.[6]

---

[3] Karl Marx criticized Adam Smith for omitting fixed capital, or "constant capital," from his treatment of costs. William Whewell (1829), applying algebra to Ricardo's theory, formulated the notion of assets as time-dated quantities of labor input. This interpretation paved the way for vertically integrated accounting models. For detailed references, see William Whewell, *Six Lectures on Political Economy*, Cambridge University Press, 1862, and Giuliana Campanelli, "Whewell's Contribution to Economic Analysis," *The Manchester School*, Vol. 50, 1982.

[4] The SEC does **not** require exchange-listed corporations—including the 71 analyzed here—to disclose the **components** of COGS (e.g., purchases of raw materials/intermediates/finished goods, or direct labor). For commercial and industrial registrants, Regulation S-X Rule 5–03 calls for a single line— "costs and expenses applicable to sales and revenues"—not a purchase/labor breakdown. By contrast, the IRS's Form 1125-A requires filers to report beginning inventory, purchases, direct labor, §263A costs, other costs, and ending inventory. In addition, period-to-period inventory valuation effects flow through COGS—e.g., LIFO liquidations and lower-of-cost/NRV write-downs—so COGS mixes direct costs with inventory holding gains/losses ("inventory profits"), further obscuring the underlying input cost structure.

[5] COGS denotes cost of goods sold; XSGA denotes selling, general and administrative expenses. Reporting varies across corporations: some embed depreciation, depletion, and amortization (DP) in COGS or XSGA; others report DP separately. Compustat normalizes these differences by recording DP separately and leaving XSGA as operating expenses excluding DP. This normalization depends on what issuers disclose in the footnotes and how reliably those items are mapped; incomplete or ambiguous disclosures can affect the split between DP and XSGA.

[6] As a professional economist trained in corporate accounting audits, I have reviewed **IRS Form 1120** filings for over 30 years. The latitude filers have in allocating costs between **COGS** (reported on **Form 1125-A**) and **XSGA** (reported among **Form 1120** deductions) is substantial. Examining COGS or XSGA **in isolation** is therefore unreliable; I combine them as **XOPR ≡ COGS + XSGA**.

Tax-book reconciliation runs through **Schedule M-1** (or **Schedule M-3** for large filers); **Schedule M-2** is an analysis of **unappropriated retained earnings**, not the primary reconciliation. These schedules and "other deductions" attachments often include **negative amounts** (contra deductions/reclassifications) that affect taxable income. Such entries can reflect recoveries, inventory valuation effects, or reclassifications and do **not** by themselves reveal whether the underlying income is **operating** or **nonoperating**. This is another reason to rely on the aggregated **XOPR** measure rather than line-by-line COGS or XSGA.

2.2 Regression Analysis Framework (1950–2024)

To quantify the long-run cost-to-revenue relationship, I estimate the reduced-form equation:

$$REVT = \lambda_0 + \lambda_1\, XOPR + \lambda_2\, PPI \tag{2.1}$$

where revenue (REVT) as a function of XOPR, with λ_1 representing the partial operating profit markup coefficient. The data spans from 1950 to 2024 and covers 71 US corporations.

The regression estimation employs the OLS with Newey-West standard errors, which minimizes the influence of residual error anomalies. This method is suitable for data with potential heteroskedasticity or serial correlations across corporations and periods.

Exhibit 2.1 provides an overview of the regression analysis performed on 71 US corporations from 1950 to 2024.

2.3 Key Findings

The regression results reveal consistent patterns across corporations and decades, highlighting structural features of total cost behavior and the operating profit markup (or operating profit margin) that reinforce my empirical model and challenge standard economic assumptions.

2.4 Intercepts

Roughly half of the companies exhibit statistically significant intercepts (denoted "Y" on Exhibit 2.1 and other related exhibits), while the remainder are statistically insignificant (denoted "N"). This intercept heterogeneity implies that corporations' fixed cost structures vary significantly.[7]

2.5 Slope Coefficients Are High and Time Invariant

The slope coefficients λ_1, representing the markup on operating costs, are high and widely dispersed across companies. The persistence and variation of these profit markups, even across corporations within the same industry, challenge the idea of

[7] Mueller himself emphasized the time-invariant nature of markup behavior. His analysis, however, focused on the AR(1) ratio of net profits after interest payments to total assets—a framing that lacks the structural cost component emphasized here. This mixing operating and nonoperating activities is also adopted by Gschwandtner.

inter-corporation or interindustry profit convergence. These differences are highlighted in the histogram fitted with the Burr XII (Singh-Maddala) curve discussed in the appendix to this book.

This empirical finding aligns with the hypothesis that corporate operating profits are persistent over the long run, surviving multiple business cycles, because of the management ability to pass through cost increases via increased prices.

2.6 High Adjusted R^2 Values Signal Good Fit

Across all companies, the regression models yield exceptionally high adjusted R^2 ($\underline{R}^2$) values, typically exceeding 0.99. The models reveal a stable and linear relationship between operating costs and revenue.

The strength of this linear association reinforces the robustness of the cost-based framework. Rather than relying on lagged dependent variables or stochastic error propagation, this model emphasizes tangible economic inputs (costs) as the explanatory mechanism for revenue generation.

2.7 Implications for Economic Modeling and Profit Analysis

The persistence of high, diverse markup coefficients across decades and sectors challenges traditional expectations of competitive profit ratio convergence and "brilliant" CEO prowers.

For example, George Stigler posited (without proof or empirical support) profit ratio (ROA) convergence in his book, *Capital and Rates of Return in Manufacturing Industries* (Princeton University Press, 1963). Stigler asserted a classical equalization claim: "There is no more important proposition in economic theory than that, under competition, the rate of return on investment tends toward equality in all industries" (p. 54) and treated it as a corollary of competition—**many firms** with **free entry/exit** (p. 55). Empirically, his "rate of return" (ROA) is built from industry-level aggregated IRS corporate tax returns and defined as **returns to all capital holders** (interest + dividends + retained earnings − income taxes, adjusting for intercorporate dividends) divided by total assets excluding investments in other companies; the income figures may not represent book values. He then examines the frequency distribution and dispersion of these industry rates (1938–1957) and their relation to industry concentration, rather than demonstrating convergence to a single, economy-wide profit rate norm.

Stigler's theoretical claim is the classical equalization of the rate of **return on investment** (a pure number) under competition (his Ch. 3, pp. 54–55); however, he measures an industry **rate of return on total assets.**[8] Knowledge of corporate accounting reveals that the acquisition or the disposition of tangible or intangible assets triggers a tax event, and assets (stock variables) do not flow among corporations or industries like larva.[9]

My theoretical and empirical findings suggest a more robust approach to modeling corporate operating profits, considering cost structures and corporate-level behavioral consistency over time.

2.8 Next Steps

Future chapters will go into individual regression profiles, exploring case-by-case patterns in intercepts and slope coefficients of Eq. (1.2 same as 2.1) fitted with historical XOPR and REVT of individual corporations.

Exhibit 2.1 Regression analysis of operating profit markup (1950–2024) ($REVT = \lambda_0 + \lambda_1\, XOPR + \lambda_2\, PPI$)

GVKEY	Companies	SIC Code	Count	λ_0	λ_1	t-Stat (λ_1)	$\underline{R}^2$
007435	3M	2670	75	Y	1.511	45.3	0.999
001078	Abbott	3845	75	N	1.437	27.2	0.998
012540	Adobe	7370	40	Y	1.73	33.3	0.997
005018	Aerojet Rocketdyne	3760	73	N	1.104	67.8	0.994
001209	Air Products & Chemicals	2810	75	Y	1.123	11	0.993
160,329	Alphabet	7370	23	N	1.493	40.4	0.997
064768	Amazon	5961	30	Y	1.153	59.5	0.998
001161	AMD	3674	53	Y	1.352	37.5	0.993
001517	American Motors	3711	37	Y	1.156	27.4	0.997
001690	Apple	3663	45	N	1.469	46.7	0.999
001704	Applied Materials	3553	53	Y	1.579	30.5	0.996
001794	Ashland	2820	75	N	1.035	117.4	0.997
001913	Avery Dennison	2670	65	N	1.143	48	0.999

continued

[8] Stigler's industry "rate of return" = (interest + dividends + retained earnings − corporate income taxes, adjusted for intercorporate dividends) ÷ total assets (book, excluding investments in other companies). By contrast, my equation (1.1) targets the **operating** margin/markup (REVT vs. XOPR), excluding nonoperating items such as depreciation and amortization, which avoids accounting effects from acquisition intangibles and other book-value judgments.

[9] Debates about the **asset base** for profit-rate measures should not be confused with ideal "putty" or "putty-clay" capital models. Those are vintage-capital assumptions about how flexible or fluid capital is before vs. after installation (recorded on a corporation's balance sheet); they are useful in growth and investment theory but do **not** resolve how to construct an empirical denominator for corporate profit rates (e.g., historical vs. replacement cost, net vs. gross stock, treatment of intangibles).

GVKEY	Companies	SIC Code	Count	λ_0	λ_1	t-Stat (λ_1)	$\underline{R}^2$
002086	Baxter	2834	75	N	1.281	15.3	0.994
002285	Boeing	3721	75	N	1.171	28	0.993
002403	Bristol-Myers	2834	75	N	1.845	13.8	0.985
002435	Brown-Forman	2085	74	Y	1.222	8.1	0.991
002817	Caterpillar	3531	75	N	1.302	37.2	0.997
162,254	Celanese	2860	22	Y	1.019	17.5	0.974
002991	Chevron	2911	65	N	1.225	43.2	0.998
020779	Cisco	3576	36	N	1.3	21.2	0.995
003091	Clark Equipment	3531	45	Y	1.13	44.7	0.996
003144	Coca-Cola	2086	75	N	1.367	19.5	0.997
008549	ConocoPhillips	1311	75	Y	1.122	50.9	0.995
003650	Cummins	3510	75	Y	1.195	140.9	1.000
003662	Curtiss-Wright	3728	75	Y	1.21	60.2	0.998
178,672	CVR Energy	2911	19	N	1.104	23.8	0.983
003734	Dana	3714	75	Y	1.112	37.3	0.997
003835	Deere & Co.	3523	75	Y	1.434	18.9	0.995
004060	Dupont de Nemours	3679	75	N	1.128	35.8	0.996
005074	EDS	7370	40	N	1.106	43.5	0.997
006730	Eli Lilly	2834	64	N	1.549	11.7	0.990
004503	Exxon	2911	75	N	1.246	33.8	0.997
004839	Ford Motor	3711	70	Y	1.27	20.7	0.995
005046	General Dynamics	3721	65	Y	1.157	111.7	0.999
005073	General Motors	3711	75	N	1.1	27.5	0.992
005234	Goodyear Tire & Rubber	3011	75	N	1.021	35.3	0.998
001380	Hess	1311	56	Y	1.137	51.7	0.986
005667	HF Sinclair	2911	64	N	1.111	77.5	0.998
001300	Honeywell International	9997	75	Y	1.135	16.7	0.995
005606	HP	3570	73	N	1.143	69.9	0.999
162,401	Huntsman	2860	23	Y	1.139	78.8	0.991
006066	IBM	7370	69	N	1.165	27.8	0.994
006008	Intel	3674	54	N	1.86	9.4	0.957
006266	Johnson & Johnson	2834	75	N	1.601	60.3	0.999
006435	Kimberly-Clark Corp	2621	75	N	1.321	69.2	0.999
005492	L3Harris	2812	67	Y	1.205	97	0.999
006774	Lockheed Martin	3760	75	N	1.184	47.3	0.999
007017	Marathon Oil[1]	1311	32	N	1.147	10.6	0.998
007017	Marathon Oil[2]	1311	36	Y	1.095	79.1	0.994
007257	Merck	2834	75	Y	1.308	13.6	0.990
012141	Microsoft	7372	40	N	2.089	9.9	0.981
162,129	Mosaic	2870	23	N	1.705	9.0	0.958
007620	Murphy Oil	1311	64	Y	1.077	113.6	0.993
6081	Navistar International	3711	71	N	1.084	51.7	0.995
007985	Northrop	3812	64	Y	1.106	47.9	0.999

GVKEY	Companies	SIC Code	Count	λ_0	λ_1	t-Stat (λ_1)	$\underline{R}^2$
117,768	Nvidia	3674	29	Y	2.996	14.0	0.976
008068	Occidental Petroleum	1311	65	Y	0.778	6.8	0.679
012142	Oracle	7370	40	N	1.758	14.9	0.995
008214	Owens Corning	3290	74	N	1.181	10.5	0.992
022447	Par Pacific Holdings	2911	36	Y	1.078	65.2	0.997
008479	PepsiCo	2080	73	N	1.223	47.2	0.999
008530	Pfizer	2834	75	N	1.713	42.5	0.988
008247	PPG Industries	2851	73	N	1.092	20.5	0.999
008762	Procter & Gamble	2840	73	N	1.334	27.5	0.997
008972	Raytheon	3812	70	N	1.159	25.5	0.998
010983	RTX	2724	75	Y	1.273	44.7	0.999
010519	Textron	3721	75	Y	1.249	51.9	0.997
001712	Trecora Resources	2911	46	N	1.127	46.5	0.995
002504	Unisys	7373	75	Y	1.113	88.1	0.993
015247	Valero Energy	2911	46	N	1.048	43.9	0.999
022325	Xilinx	3674	32	Y	1.274	33.4	0.990

Chapter 3
Petroleum and Natural Gas Exploration

Industry analysts categorize the petroleum industry into three major segments: upstream, midstream, and downstream. While these segments are distinct, assuming no overlap or interaction between them is unrealistic. Many corporations operate as vertically integrated conglomerates, controlling multiple parts of the supply chain.[1]

This chapter focuses on the upstream sector, specifically analyzing the operating profit markup of five major US-based corporations engaged in petroleum and natural gas exploration and production. These companies have undergone significant restructuring from 1950 to 2024, driven by mergers, acquisitions, and divestitures. As a result, the analysis concentrates on the surviving entities that represent the core of the industry's exploration capabilities.[2]

3.1 Regression Analysis and Slope Coefficients

To evaluate the relationship between revenue REVT and XOPR, I applied our reduced-form linear regression model (Eq. 1.2) to each of the five corporations.

Four of the five companies analyzed exhibited statistically significant slope coefficients, confirming a strong and consistent linear relationship between total cost

[1] In every industry during the period covered, corporations operate as vertically integrated conglomerates across various supply chain segments. Therefore, classifying oil and gas exploration companies within a specific stream is questionable.

[2] Chevron agreed to acquire Hess in an all-stock transaction on October 23, 2023. In March 2024, ExxonMobil and China National Offshore Oil Corporation (CNOOC) initiated arbitration proceedings, asserting preemptive rights over Hess's stake in Guyana's Stabroek Block. Hess shareholders approved the Chevron-Hess merger on May 28, 2024, and the Federal Trade Commission (FTC) completed its antitrust review of the merger on June 30, 2024. As of this writing, the arbitration court has ruled that Chevron may proceed with its acquisition of Hess.

E. A. Silva, *U.S. Corporate Profits, 1950–2024*, SpringerBriefs in Economics,
https://doi.org/10.1007/978-3-032-11399-3_3

and revenue. These slopes, interpreted as operating profit markups, remained consistent throughout the study.

One exception is Occidental Petroleum. The OLS with Newey-West standard errors model for this company yielded divergent slope coefficients. The analysis adopted a power function as an alternative specification in this case. The model achieved a better fit by applying a double logarithmic transformation to revenue and total costs, indicating a proportional relationship (constant returns to scale). The slope of the log-log regression approached one, further affirming structural alignment between total cost and revenue.

3.2 Intercepts and Structural Implications

Some companies demonstrated positive and statistically significant intercepts, while others did not.[3] A significant intercept implies a baseline level of total costs independent of revenue, a fixed cost structure. In contrast, insignificant intercepts suggest a tighter alignment between expenses and revenue, indicating variable cost dominance.

These differences complicate traditional ratio analyses, especially those that rely on quartiles or average markup values. When intercepts are nonzero or slopes are nonlinear, parametric summary statistics misrepresent the underlying data relationships.

3.3 Long-Run Markup Stability

The most compelling finding from this analysis is the temporal stability of the slope coefficients. Despite economic cycles, oil price shocks, and industry consolidation, the markup estimates for these corporations remained stable across decades. This stability challenges standard economic theories that expect profit rates to converge due to competition or market correction mechanisms.

This observed persistence in corporate-specific markup levels supports the idea that industry structure, barriers to entry, and product differentiation preserve profitability over time. These factors are suggestive, and not analyzed in this book.

[3] Positive and significant intercept matters for purposes of data analysis because the function may not be linear; the intercept may not be zero. The two events combined imply that statistics (quartiles, median, mean) may be misleading or unreliable.

3.4 Economic Implications

Two key implications emerge from the results:

Barriers to Entry: The persistence of high markup coefficients suggests that significant entry barriers, such as high capital requirements, regulatory constraints, and the need for advanced geological and engineering capabilities, define upstream petroleum exploration.[4]

Resilience to Market Shocks: The stability of slope coefficients during oil price volatility and geopolitical disruption periods reveals a resilient cost-to-revenue structure. These corporations manage to preserve predictable markups despite changing external conditions.[5]

Exhibit 3 presents the regression results for the five petroleum and natural gas exploration companies, detailing intercept significance, slope coefficients, *t*-statistics, and model fit ($\underline{R}^2$) for each corporation across the study period.

3.5 Summary of Findings

The regression results yield the following conclusions. Slope coefficients (i.e., operating profit markups) are significant, stable, and non-convergent. Occidental Petroleum deviates from linearity but aligns under a power function, suggesting proportional scaling. Intercepts vary across corporations, indicating diverse cost structures (some fixed, others variable).

These results support a view of the petroleum exploration sector as structured, resilient, and strategically entrenched, rather than fluid or competitive in the traditional economic sense.

Chapter 8 follows up on this analysis, where I turn to petroleum refining (the downstream phase of the supply chain) to investigate whether the same pattern of markup stability holds. In this phase, producers transform raw petroleum into finished consumer products.

[4] Joe Bain, *Barriers to New Competition*. Harvard University Press, 1956. Bain identifies several barriers to entry, including economies of large scale, product differentiation, and cost advantages.

[5] I divided Marathon Oil Corp into two periods: the first from 1950 to 1981, with an estimated operating profit markup of 1.1468 ± 0.1079, and the second from 1988 to 2023, with a markup of 1.0952 ± 0.0138. This division was prompted by the absence of paired data from 1982 to 1987. There are two distinct slope coefficients for the two periods.

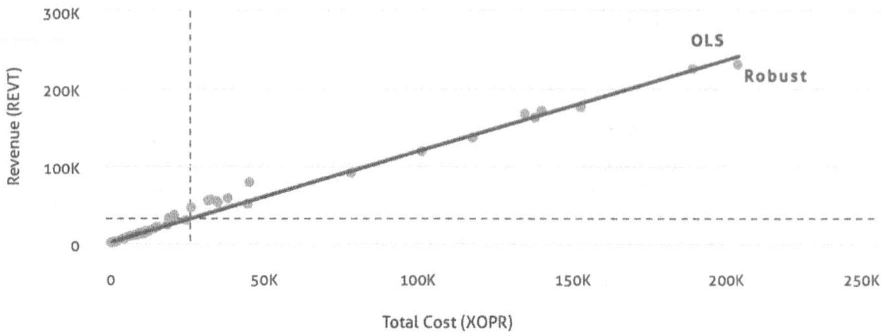

Exhibit 3.1 Conoco Philips

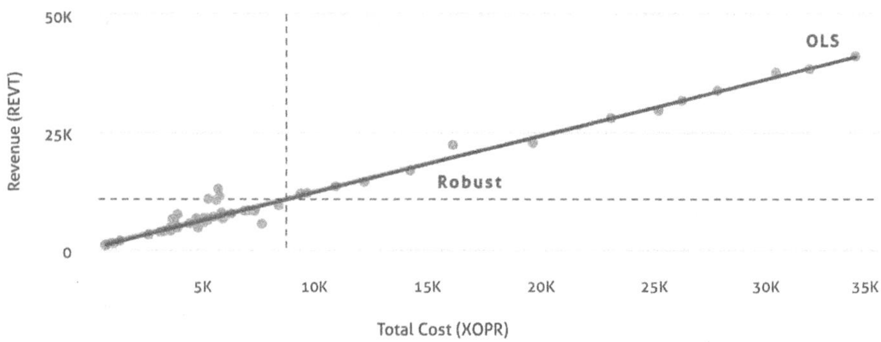

Exhibit 3.2 Hess

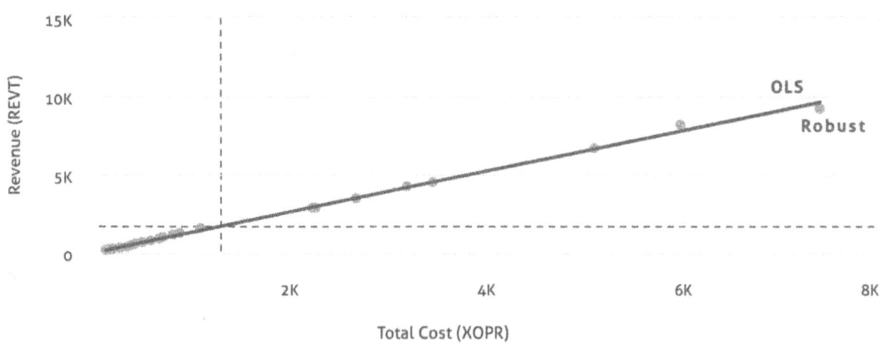

Exhibit 3.3 Marathon Oil

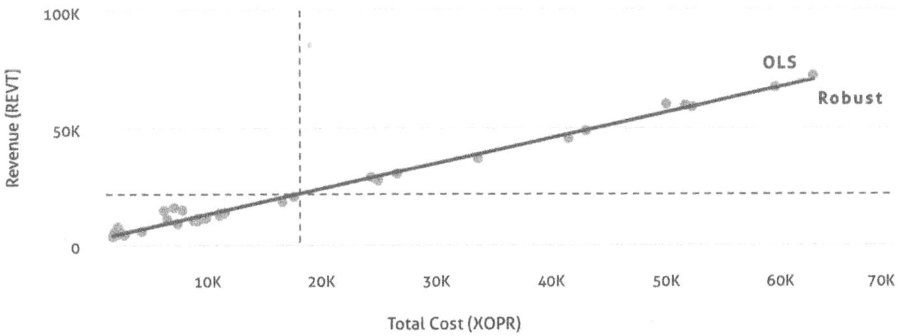

Exhibit 3.4 Marathon Oil

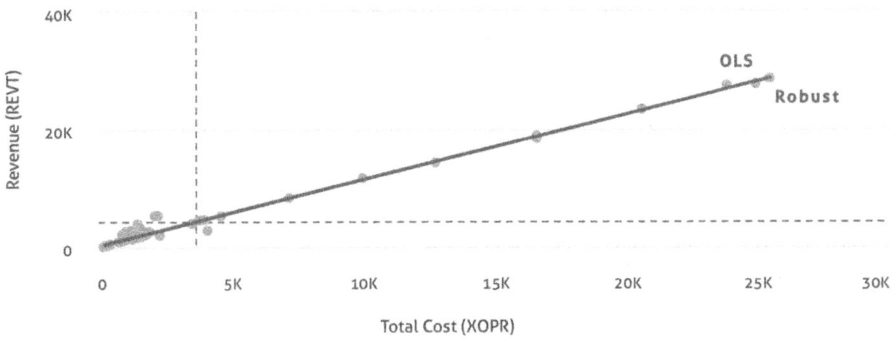

Exhibit 3.5 Murphy Oil

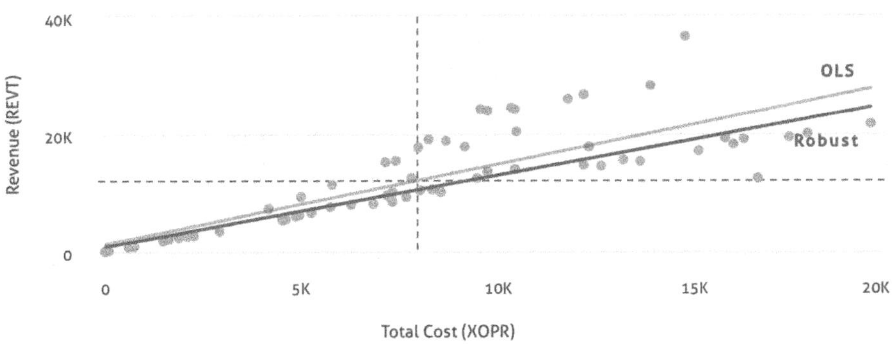

Exhibit 3.6 Occidental Petroleum

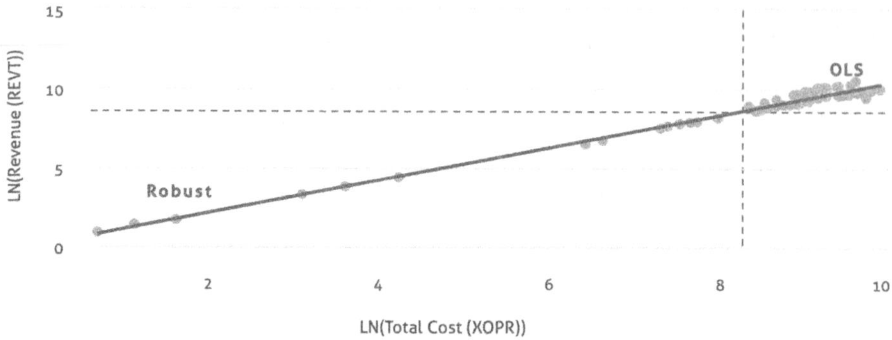

Exhibit 3.7 Occidental Petroleum

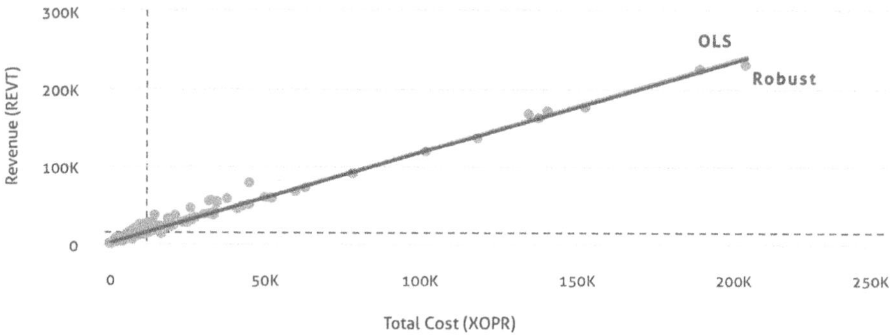

Exhibit 3.8 All companies

Exhibit 3.9 Regression summary ($REVT = \lambda_0 + \lambda_1\ XOPR + \lambda_2\ PPI$)

GVKEY	Companies	Year range	Count	λ_0	λ_1	t-Stat (λ_1)	$\underline{R}^2$
008549	ConocoPhillips	1950–2024	75	Y	1.12	50.9	0.995
001380	Hess	1969–2024	56	Y	1.14	51.7	0.986
007017	Marathon Oil	1950–1981	32	N	1.15	10.6	0.998
007017	Marathon Oil	1988–2023	36	Y	1.1	79.1	0.994
007620	Murphy Oil	1961–2024	64	Y	1.08	113.6	0.993
008068	Occidental Petroleum	1960–2024	65	Y	0.78	8.5	0.879
	All companies	*1950–2024*	*328*	*Y*	*1.15*	*74.5*	*0.988*

Chapter 4
Beverages

The US beverage industry has an oligopolistic market structure, with three major players dominating the market: Coca-Cola, PepsiCo, and Brown-Forman.[1] These corporations control a significant market share and possess substantial pricing power, deeply entrenched distribution networks, and brand recognition.

This chapter analyzes the cost-to-revenue structure of these three corporations by estimating the operating profit markup, represented by the slope coefficient λ_1.

4.1 Regression Analysis and Slope Coefficients

PepsiCo and Brown-Forman exhibit nearly identical slope coefficients, suggesting a uniform markup over operating costs across decades. Coca-Cola, by contrast, has a higher slope coefficient, pointing to a higher long-run markup on total costs.

4.2 Intercepts and Structural Implications

Brown-Forman reports a statistically significant intercept, which implies that revenues include a fixed component, a displacement from the origin in the regression model, and are not proportional to total costs. This nonzero intercept indicates that even at minimal cost levels, it maintains a baseline level of revenue.

[1] Brown-Forman brands include Jack Daniel's, Old Forester, Woodford Reserve, GlenDronach, BenRiach, Glenglassaugh, Herradura, Korbel, and Chambord.

E. A. Silva, *U.S. Corporate Profits, 1950–2024*, SpringerBriefs in Economics,
https://doi.org/10.1007/978-3-032-11399-3_4

A significant intercept complicates the interpretation of markup as a pure ratio. In a purely proportional model, markup is the slope. However, the intercept introduces a nonlinear component, distorting ratio-based summaries such as quartiles, medians, or means of operating profit ratios.[2]

4.3 Long-Run Markup Stability

The regression fit is strong for all three corporations, especially Coca-Cola and PepsiCo, both of which show high $\underline{R}^{2}$ values. These values indicate that total costs predict revenue with consistency, confirming the suitability of the regression model as a long-run predictor of corporate behavior in this sector.

The robust linearity of the markup relationship over time underscores the beverage industry's predictable cost structure. Brand loyalty, fixed distribution infrastructures, and economies of scale contribute to this consistency. Again, these factors are suggestive, and not examined in this book.

Exhibit 4.5 summarizes the regression results for Coca-Cola, PepsiCo, and Brown-Forman, including each company's intercept significance, slope coefficient (λ_1), t-statistic, and $\underline{R}^{2}$ value over the whole sample period.

4.4 Economic Implications

The observed markup stability and a significant intercept for all companies reflect a consolidated industry with substantial barriers to entry and pricing discipline. The disparity between Coca-Cola's markup and those of PepsiCo and Brown-Forman undermines the idea of markup convergence even within comparable oligopolies in similar industries.

Overall, the beverage industry demonstrates long-term profit persistence and cost control discipline that align with this study's findings: operating profit markups are stable, corporation specific, and resistant to competitive convergence.

[2] If the relationship has an intercept, then the profit ratio depends on the inverse of revenue; as revenue increases, the profit ratio shrinks.

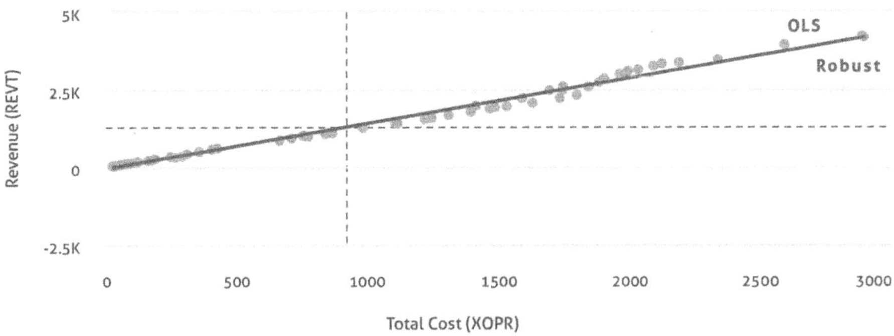

Exhibit 4.1 Brown-Forman Corp

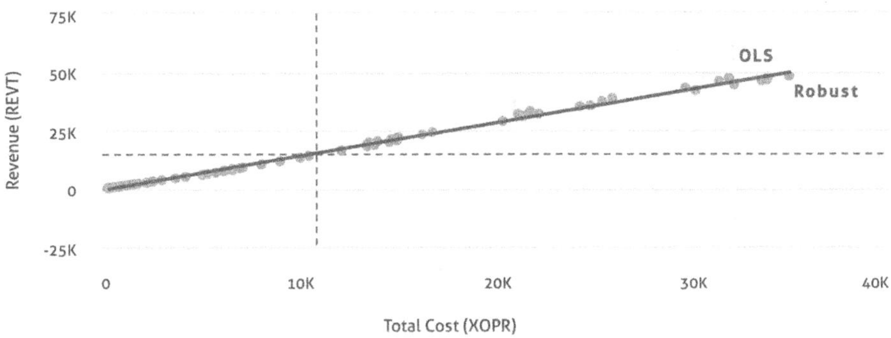

Exhibit 4.2 Coca-Cola Co (The)

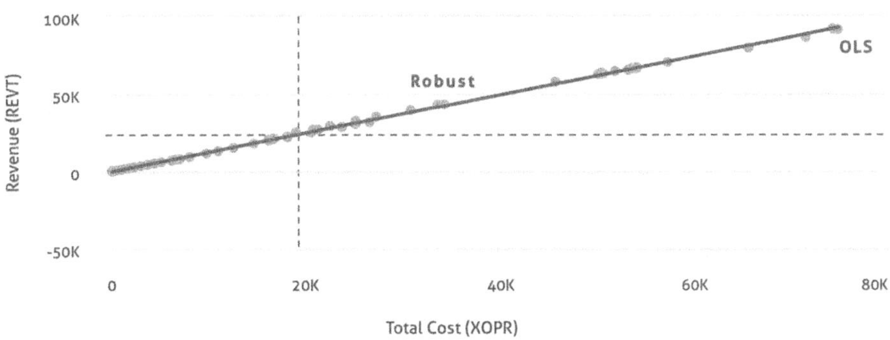

Exhibit 4.3 PepsiCo Inc.

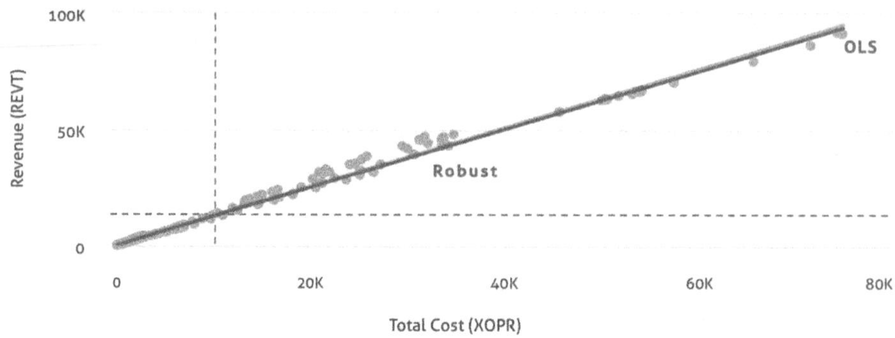

Exhibit 4.4 All companies

Exhibit 4.5 Regression summary ($REVT = \lambda_0 + \lambda_1\ XOPR + \lambda_2\ PPI$)

GVKEY	Companies	Year range	Count	λ_0	λ_1	t-Stat (λ_1)	$\underline{R}^2$
002435	Brown-Forman Corp	1951–2024	74	Y	1.22	8.1	0.991
003144	Coca-Cola co (the)	1950–2024	75	N	1.37	19.5	0.997
008479	PepsiCo Inc.	1950–2024	75	N	1.22	47.2	0.999
	All companies	*1950–2024*	*224*	*Y*	*1.23*	*57.3*	*0.995*

Chapter 5
Manufacturing

Economics emerged as a science with the rise of manufacturing, which has long served as the cornerstone of capitalism.[1] While agriculture, trade, and finance each played indispensable roles in shaping modern economic systems, the expansion of industrial production (mass production, division of labor, and mechanization) grounded economics in measurable, empirical analysis. From Adam Smith's pin factory to Marx's relative surplus value theory, manufacturing has been a conceptual scaffold for economic thought.

The United States retains a formidable industrial base, and despite periods of deindustrialization and offshoring, it retains a highly concentrated manufacturing core. This chapter examines six of the most representative corporations in this evolving landscape: 3M, Avery Dennison, Celanese, Goodyear Tire & Rubber, Kimberly-Clark Corp, and Owens Corning.[2]

5.1 Operating Profit Markup by Regression Analysis

I apply our reduced-form model (Eq. 1.2) to estimate the long-run relationship between revenue REVT and XOPR for each corporation. As with prior chapters, XOPR encompasses COGS and XSGA, offering a comprehensive picture of

[1] Capitalism is an economic system in which the two primary sources of income are wages and salaries and enterprise profits. The capitalist economic structure can coexist with various political superstructures, including both elected and authoritarian regimes.

[2] Manufacturing employment in the United States has changed over the course of the observation period. Total civilian employment has grown from 57.63 million in January 1950 to 163.97 million in April 2025. As a percent of total civilian employment, manufacturing employment has fallen from an observation period maximum of 26.8% in May 1953 to an observation period minimum of 7.8% in January 2025. See Appendix 3.

E. A. Silva, *U.S. Corporate Profits, 1950–2024*, SpringerBriefs in Economics,
https://doi.org/10.1007/978-3-032-11399-3_5

corporate-level cost structures. The slope coefficient λ_1 captures the long-run markup on total operating costs. The slope coefficients derived from these regressions vary within the same industry. 3M achieves a high operating profit markup, suggesting a substantial surplus generated per cost unit. At the opposite end of the spectrum, Celanese and Goodyear Tire & Rubber register the lowest markups among the six corporations.

5.2 Intercepts and Structural Implications

I pay close attention to slope coefficients and the significance of the intercepts. A statistically insignificant intercept implies a proportional relationship between costs and revenues.

3M and Celanese are notable exceptions. The regression reports statistically significant intercepts, suggesting a baseline level of revenue even at zero reported operating cost. The presence of a significant intercept also cautions against naïve ratio analyses, which assume pure proportionality.

5.3 Oligopoly and Profit Differentials

The disparities in the operating profit markup across these six corporations are consistent with broader theories of oligopolistic behavior. As Sylos-Labini (1969) discussed, corporations with differentiated products and strong brand identity are more likely to secure stable profit markups and resist competitive erosion. 3M and Owens Corning operate in specialized markets with patented technologies and industrial niches. Avery Dennison, a major supplier of pressure-sensitive materials and RFID labels, leverages global scale and innovation in packaging technologies.

5.4 Regression Strength

Across the six corporations, the regressions yield high $\underline{R}^2$ values, ranging from 0.974 (Celanese) to 0.999 (3 M, Avery Dennison, and Kimberly-Clark Corp). These values underscore the strong predictive power of total costs in estimating revenue. The models demonstrate a linear and stable relationship, validating the use of the reduced-form equation as an appropriate tool for long-term profitability analysis.

This pattern aligns with findings from the previous chapter: operating profit markups appear structurally embedded and corporation specific. They defy expectations of convergence across corporations, even within similar industries.

5.5 Summary and Observations

The results from the manufacturing sector reinforce several key themes.

Corporation-Specific Cost Structures. Even within a similar industry, profit markups vary widely, shaped by product differentiation, vertical integration, and market power.

Predictive Power of Costs. Total operating expenses (XOPR) remain the most reliable predictor of revenue over a multi-decade time frame.

Limited Convergence. Despite economic theories predicting competitive equalization of profit rates, empirical data show that corporations like 3M maintain persistent advantages, while others like Goodyear operate under tighter constraints.

Role of Product Differentiation. Consistent with Sylos-Labini's oligopoly theory, higher markups correlate with greater control over pricing and market segmentation.

Exhibit 5.8 summarizes the regression results for the six representative manufacturing corporations, highlighting intercept significance, long-run markup (slope λ_1), t-statistics, and $\underline{R}^2$ values. These results reflect each corporation's structural cost dynamics and profitability patterns over the long term.

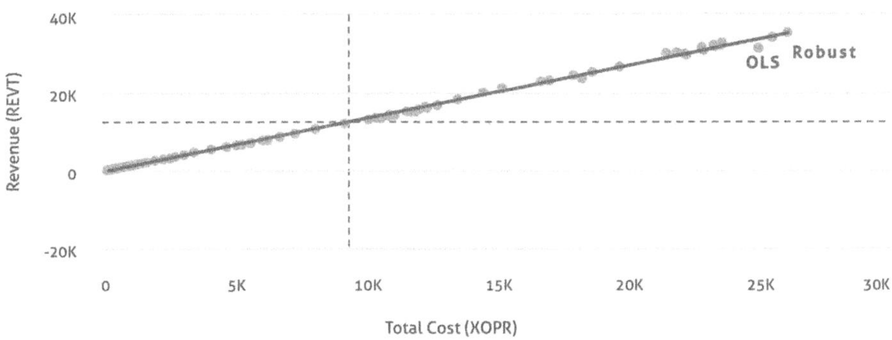

Exhibit 5.1 3M

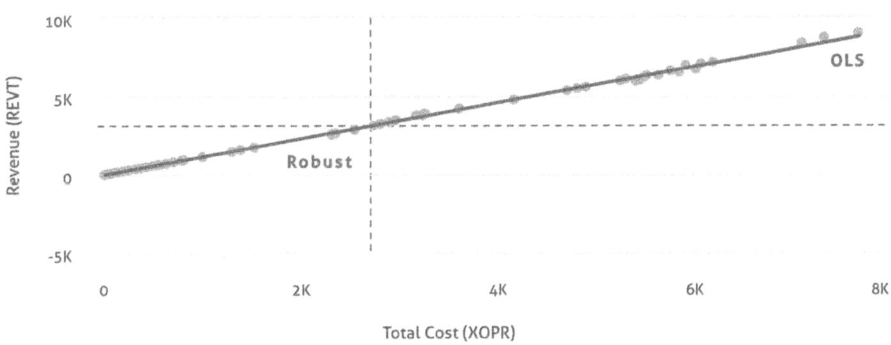

Exhibit 5.2 Avery Dennison

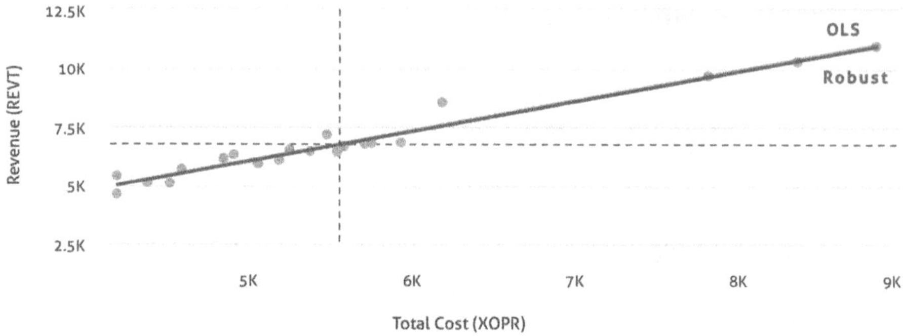

Exhibit 5.3 Celanese

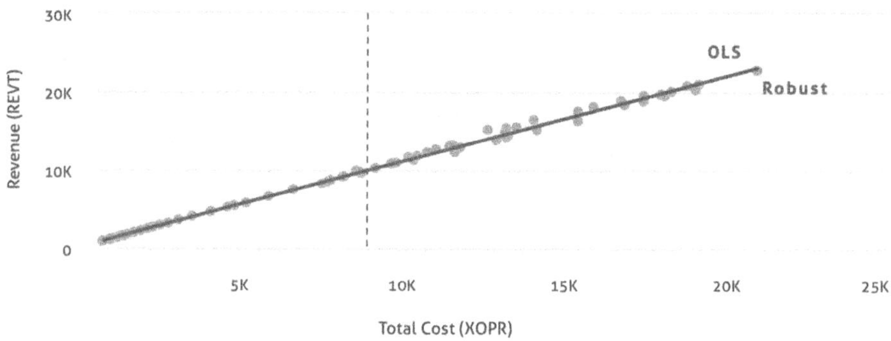

Exhibit 5.4 Goodyear Tire & Rubber

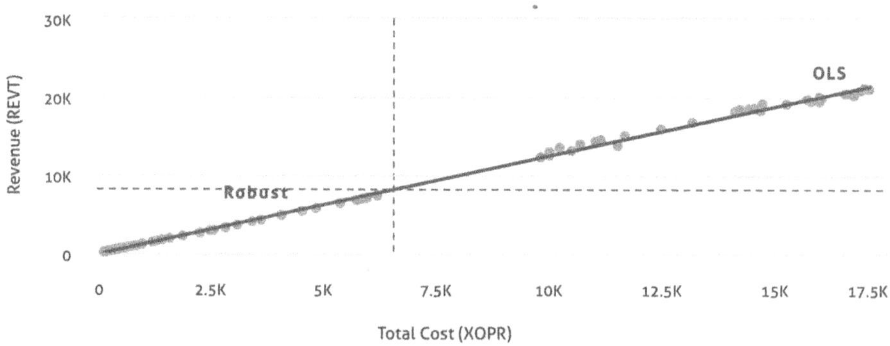

Exhibit 5.5 Kimberly-Clark Corp

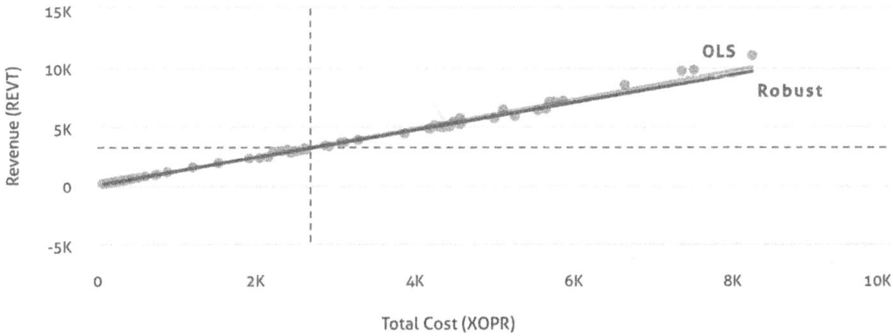

Exhibit 5.6 Owens Corning

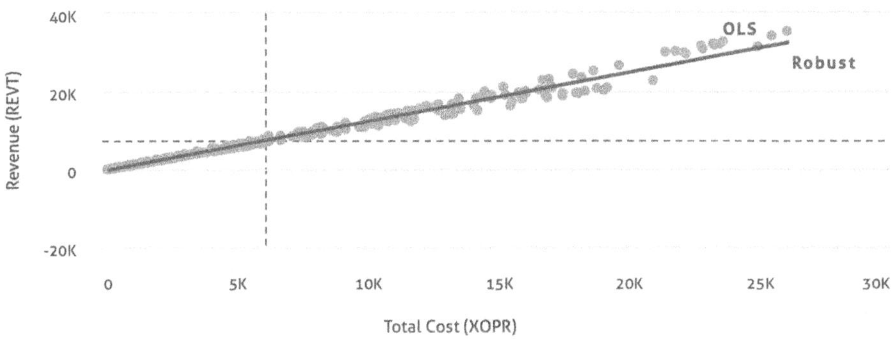

Exhibit 5.7 All companies

Exhibit 5.8 Regression summary ($REVT = \lambda_0 + \lambda_1 XOPR + \lambda_2 PPI$)

GVKEY	Companies	Year range	Count	λ_0	λ_1	t-Stat (λ_1)	R^2
007435	3 M	1950–2024	75	Y	1.51	45.3	0.999
001913	Avery Dennison	1960–2024	65	N	1.14	48	0.999
162,254	Celanese	2003–2024	22	Y	1.02	17.5	0.974
005234	Goodyear Tire & Rubber	1950–2024	75	N	1.02	35.3	0.998
006435	Kimberly-Clark Corp	1950–2024	75	N	1.32	69.2	0.999
008214	Owens Corning	1951–2024	74	N	1.18	10.5	0.992
	All companies	*1950–2024*	*386*	*N*	*1.29*	*29.5*	*0.986*

Chapter 6
Pharmaceutical

The pharmaceuticals industry represents another oligopoly, distinct in its reliance on two primary sources of intangibles: research and development (which generates manufacturing intangibles) and advertising, promotion, and detailing (which yield marketing intangibles). These twin pillars, innovation and influence, differentiate the pharmaceutical sector from other manufacturing-intensive industries and create a complex structural profile.

This chapter examines seven of the largest and most influential US-based pharmaceutical corporations: Abbott, Baxter, Bristol-Myers, Johnson & Johnson, Eli Lilly, Merck, and Pfizer. Entry into this sector is restricted by capital expenditures (CAPX) and the need for scientific expertise, government approval, and long-term investment in R&D pipelines.

6.1 Operating Profit Markup

Using the reduced-form equation (1.2), I estimate the long-run markup coefficients λ_1 for each corporation. These slope coefficients represent the operating profit markup before depreciation and amortization and offer a structural measure of cost-efficiency and revenue generation over time.

The regression results reveal a substantial spread in markup performance among the seven pharmaceutical corporations. Baxter exhibits the lowest markup, suggesting tighter cost constraints in its operating model. Bristol-Myers Squibb reports the highest markup, underscoring the profitability achievable through successful patent protection, blockbuster drugs, and scale advantages in global distribution.

E. A. Silva, *U.S. Corporate Profits, 1950–2024*, SpringerBriefs in Economics,
https://doi.org/10.1007/978-3-032-11399-3_6

6.2 Intercepts and Cost Structure Variance

The regression intercepts further reveal the heterogeneity of cost structures across the industry. All corporations except Merck show statistically insignificant intercepts, implying that their cost-revenue relationship is primarily proportional. Merck exhibits a statistically significant intercept, indicating the presence of baseline revenue or fixed-cost coverage even when operating expenses are near zero. The variation in intercept significance complicates ratio-based summaries and supports the continued use of regression-based markups as the appropriate metric for long-run profitability analysis.

6.3 Regression Strength

All regression equations yield high $\underline{R}^2$ values, exceeding 0.985 across the sample. These strong fits indicate that XOPR is a highly predictive determinant of revenue in the pharmaceutical sector. The consistency and linearity of these relationships validate the regression model as a suitable model of cost-to-revenue dynamics over the long term.

6.4 Vertical Integration and Intangibles

Pharmaceutical companies demonstrate a high degree of vertical integration, comparable to upstream petroleum. These corporations control nearly every aspect of their production process, from the synthesis of active pharmaceutical ingredients (APIs) to the manufacture, packaging, and global distribution of finished goods. A defining characteristic of the sector is its intensive R&D investment, often accounting for 15–20% of annual revenue.[1] Without these continual investments, corporations risk obsolescence or profit erosion.

6.5 Strategic Marketing and Detailing

Profitability in this industry also hinges on advertising and promotion, especially in markets like the United States, where direct-to-consumer advertising is permitted. Pharmaceutical corporations engage in "detailing," a medical outreach targeted at healthcare professionals, designed to influence prescription patterns.

---

[1] Research and development in the pharmaceutical industry. (2021, April 1). Congressional Budget Office. https://www.cbo.gov/publication/57126

These strategic campaigns reinforce brand identity and increase product uptake, enabling corporations to defend or expand market share even in saturated therapeutic classes. Detailing, in combination with mass media marketing, contributes to the high operating margins observed across the sector.

6.6 Summary and Observations

The pharmaceutical sector combines high operating profit markups and structural entry barriers, making it a paradigmatic example of a profit-persistent oligopoly. While intercept significance varies, slope coefficients remain consistently high, reinforcing that operating profit behavior in this industry is corporation specific and resistant to convergence. Under a more participatory political regime–one in which the public interest has a real voice–the pharmaceutical industry's high operating profits would be treated like utilities and subjected to explicit profit limits.

Exhibit 6.9 presents the regression results for seven major pharmaceutical corporations, summarizing intercept significance, markup coefficients (λ_1), t-statistics, and $\underline{R}^2$ values.

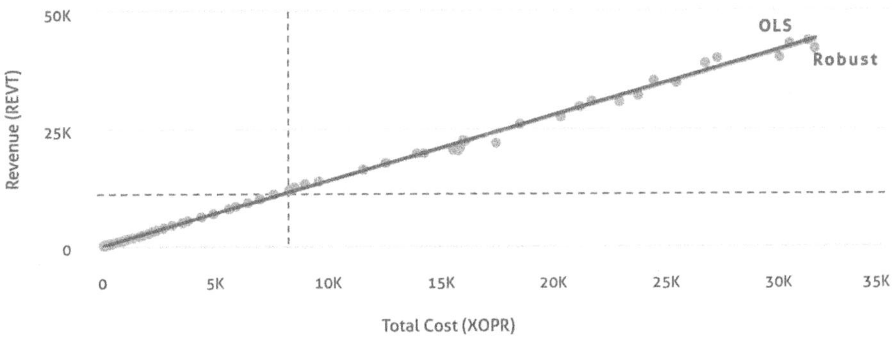

Exhibit 6.1 Abbott Laboratories

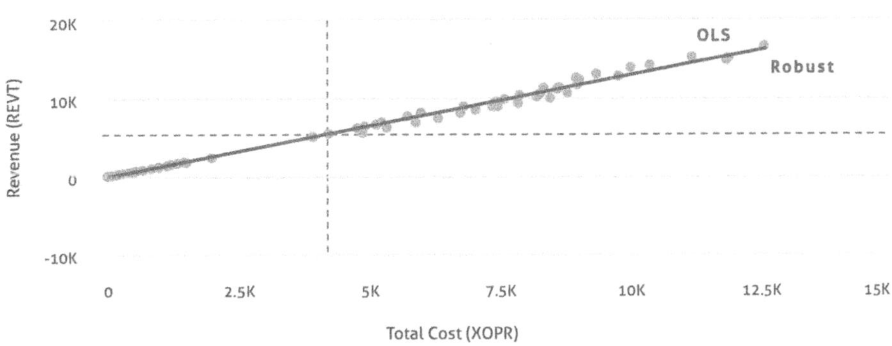

Exhibit 6.2 Baxter International Inc.

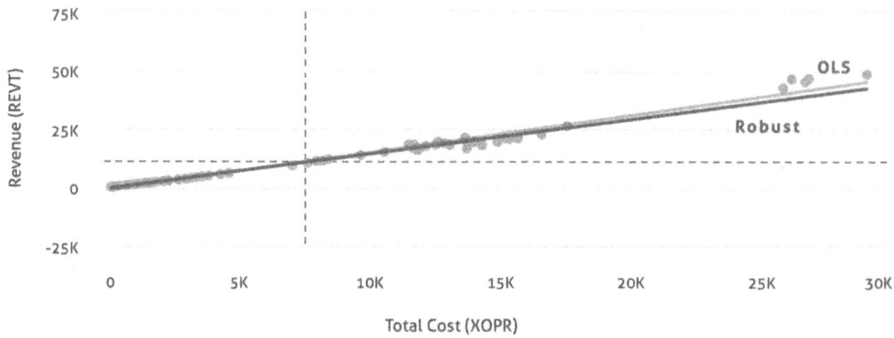

Exhibit 6.3 Bristol-Myers Squibb Co

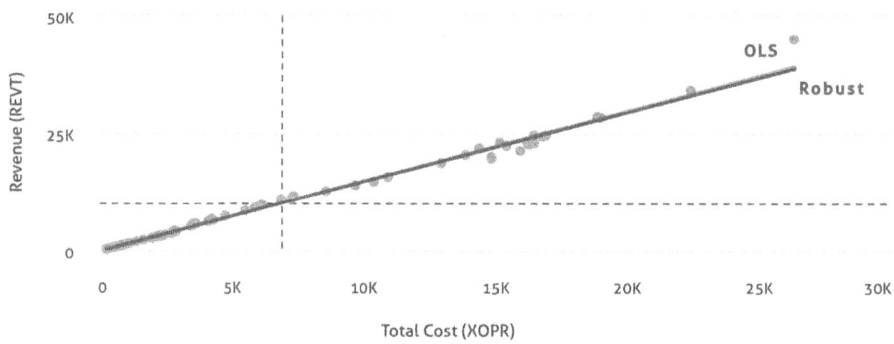

Exhibit 6.4 Eli Lilly and Co

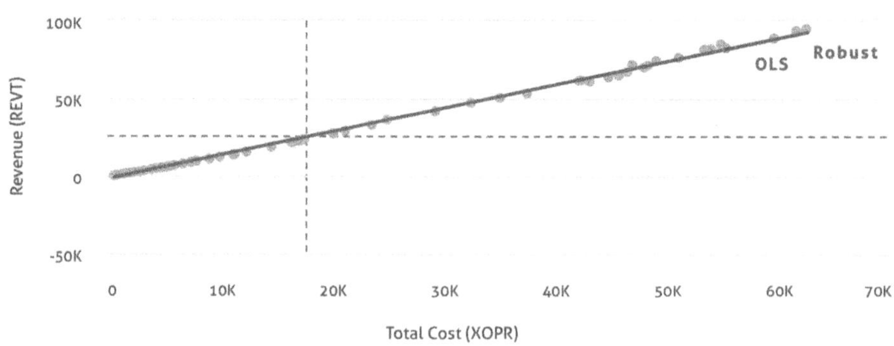

Exhibit 6.5 Johnson & Johnson

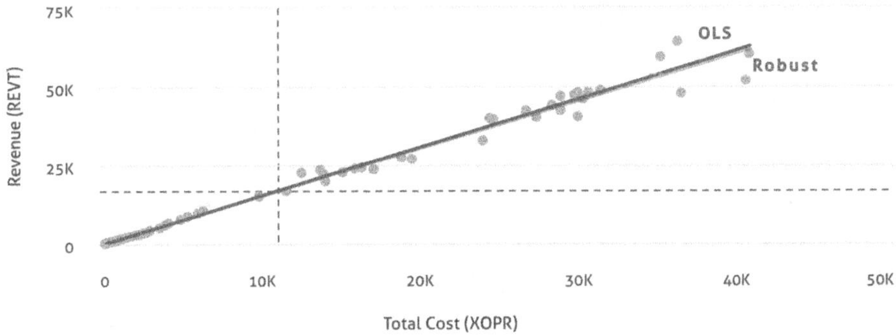

Exhibit 6.6 Merck & Co Inc.

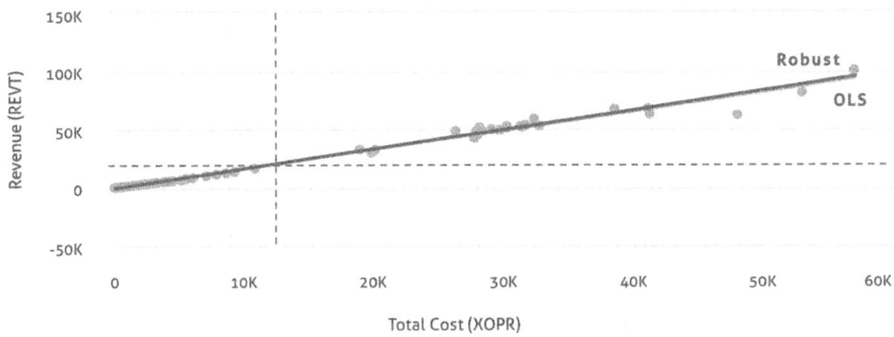

Exhibit 6.7 Pfizer Inc.

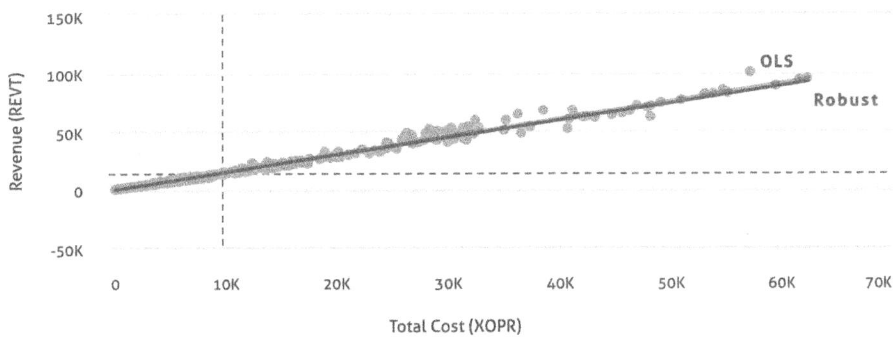

Exhibit 6.8 All companies

Exhibit 6.9 Regression summary ($REVT = \lambda_0 + \lambda_1\ XOPR + \lambda_2\ PPI$)

GVKEY	Companies	Year range	Count	λ_0	λ_1	t-Stat (λ_1)	$\underline{R}^2$
001078	Abbott laboratories	1950–2024	75	N	1.44	27.2	0.998
002086	Baxter international Inc.	1950–2024	75	N	1.28	15.3	0.994
002403	Bristol-Myers Squibb co	1950–2024	75	N	1.84	13.8	0.985
006266	Johnson & Johnson	1950–2024	75	N	1.6	60.3	0.999
006730	Eli Lilly and co	1961–2024	64	N	1.55	11.7	0.990
007257	Merck & co Inc.	1950–2024	75	Y	1.31	13.6	0.990
008530	Pfizer Inc.	1950–2024	75	N	1.71	42.5	0.988
	All companies	*1950–2024*	*514*	*N*	*1.55*	*49.2*	*0.989*

Chapter 7
Chemicals and Allied Products

The chemicals industry is at the intersection of raw material transformation and advanced industrial applications. It shares operational and structural characteristics with the petroleum and pharmaceutical sectors. Like them, it is dominated by oligopolies—large, vertically integrated corporations with extensive global operations and proprietary technologies. These corporations produce industrial gases, specialty polymers, agricultural fertilizers and consumer household products.

This chapter analyzes seven leading corporations within the chemicals and allied products sector: Air Products & Chemicals, Ashland, DuPont de Nemours, Huntsman, Mosaic, PPG Industries, and Procter & Gamble. Each operates with distinct cost structures, product mixes, and degrees of vertical integration. What binds them is their shared reliance on high fixed costs, economies of scale, and long investment cycles.

7.1 Operating Profit Markup

As in previous chapters, I apply our reduced-form model (Eq. 1.2) to estimate the operating profit markup, represented by the slope coefficient λ_1, which is the sum of COGS and XSGA, capturing all direct and indirect operational expenditures.

The slope coefficients across the seven chemical companies demonstrate significant variation, from 3% to 71%. Ashland reports the lowest markup, while Mosaic, a major fertilizer and agricultural chemical producer, achieves the highest markup, illustrating substantial leverage and pricing power in its segment.

Air Products & Chemicals, DuPont De Nemours, and Huntsman fall into a middle range, with markups of 12%, 13%, and 14%, respectively. Their results confirm that diversified chemical production and strong brand identity (in the case of DuPont De Nemours) contribute to long-run profitability.

E. A. Silva, *U.S. Corporate Profits, 1950–2024*, SpringerBriefs in Economics,
https://doi.org/10.1007/978-3-032-11399-3_7

7.2 Intercepts

The regression intercepts reveal meaningful differences in corporate cost architecture. Most companies exhibit statistically insignificant intercepts, suggesting a tighter coupling between expenses and revenues, an operational mode in which variable costs dominate and economies of scale play a reduced role.

Statistically insignificant intercepts imply that fixed costs are negligible. This suggests a linear relationship between revenue and total operating expenses and reinforces the validity of relying on λ_1 as a reliable indicator of profitability across corporations.

7.3 Regression Results

The regression model applied across the seven corporations returns strong statistical fits, with $\underline{R}^2$ values consistently exceeding 0.95. These results confirm the reliability of total operating expenses as a predictor of revenue. The linear cost-to-revenue relationship remains stable across decades of operational and macroeconomic change.

This regression consistency reinforces a recurring theme of this book: that long-term profitability, when expressed through reduced-form regressions, is predictable, stable, and resistant to convergence. No evidence emerges to support the standard hypothesis of inter-corporation markup alignment, even within a closely related sector such as chemicals.

7.4 Vertical Integration and Market Power

The chemicals sector exhibits notable vertical integration, especially among corporations producing upstream materials and intermediates. DuPont de Nemours, for instance, manages raw material sourcing, intermediate processing, and final product formulation across multiple industrial chains. PPG Industries integrates pigment production with coatings and surface technologies.

This integration enables oligopolies to mitigate supply disruptions and maintain pricing consistency. Procter & Gamble, while widely classified as a consumer goods company, maintains chemical production capacity for its household products, securing greater autonomy over input materials and formulation standards.

Vertical integration also strengthens barriers to entry. Corporations with end-to-end control over production pipelines enjoy efficiencies and informational advantages that protect their margins and limit exposure to commodity volatility.

7.5 Summary and Observations

Two themes emerge from the operating profit markup analysis of these seven chemical corporations. The first theme is product specialization and market differentiation. Companies with narrow product specialization and agricultural ties (e.g., Mosaic) or proprietary consumer brands (e.g., Procter & Gamble) tend to achieve higher operating markups. De novo, these considerations are suggestive, and not subject to statistical testing in this book.

The second theme is disparity in profitability across subsectors. The wide spread of markups, from Ashland's 3% to Mosaic's 71%, shows that the chemical industry does not function as a homogeneous sector.

Exhibit 7.9 presents the regression results for seven major chemical and allied product corporations. It summarizes intercept significance, slope coefficients (λ_1), t-statistics, and $\underline{R}^2$ values, highlighting each corporation's structural cost patterns and long-run markup performance.

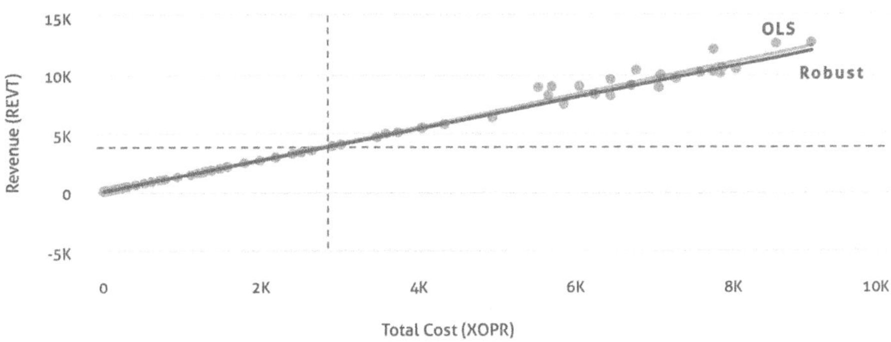

Exhibit 7.1 Air Products and Chemicals Inc.

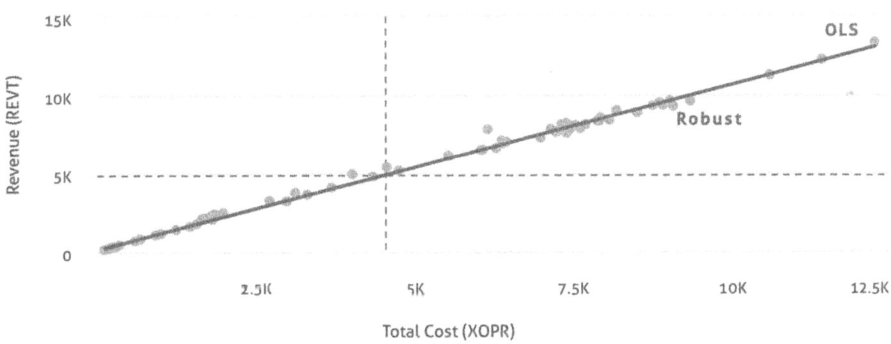

Exhibit 7.2 Ashland Inc.

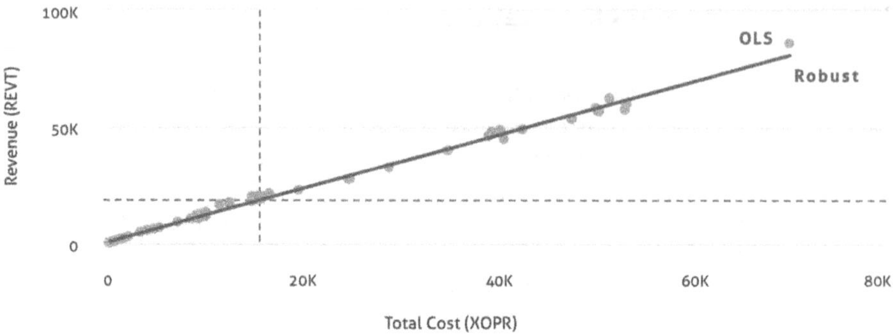

Exhibits 7.3 Dupont De Nemours Inc.

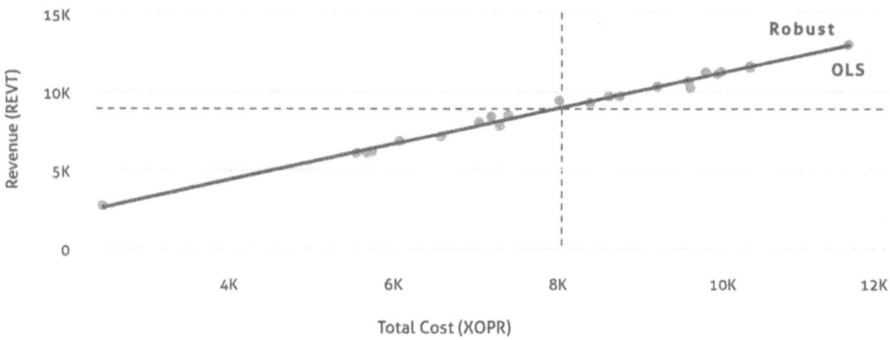

Exhibit 7.4 Huntsman Corp

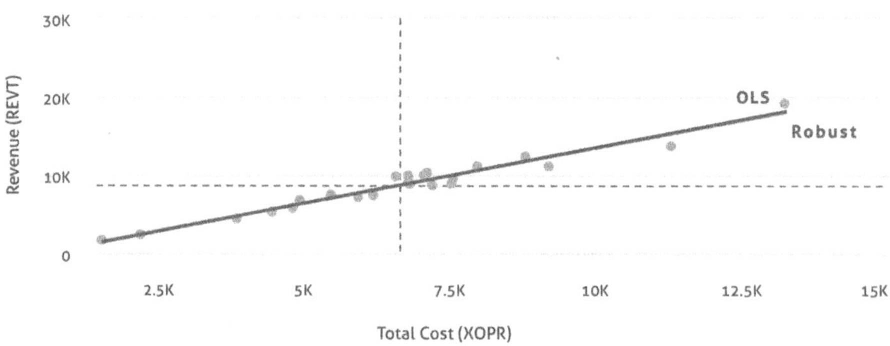

Exhibit 7.5 Mosaic Company (The)

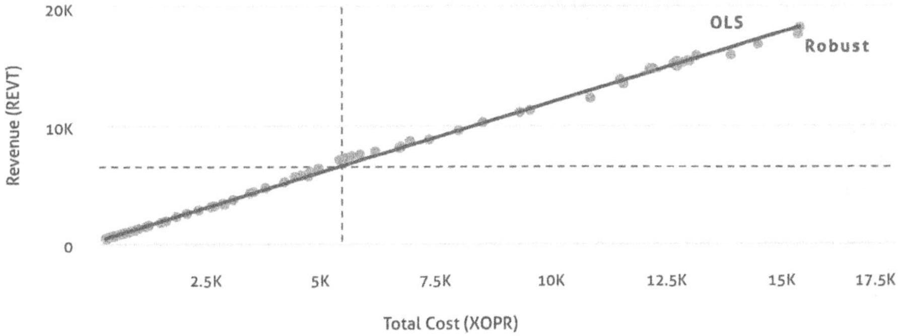

Exhibit 7.6 PPG Industries Inc.

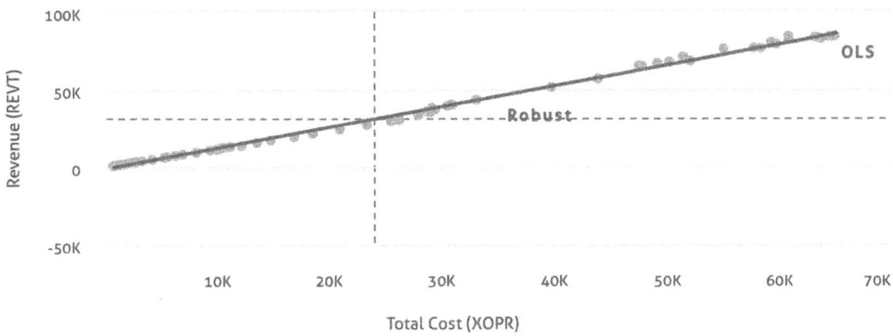

Exhibit 7.7 Procter & Gamble Co (The)

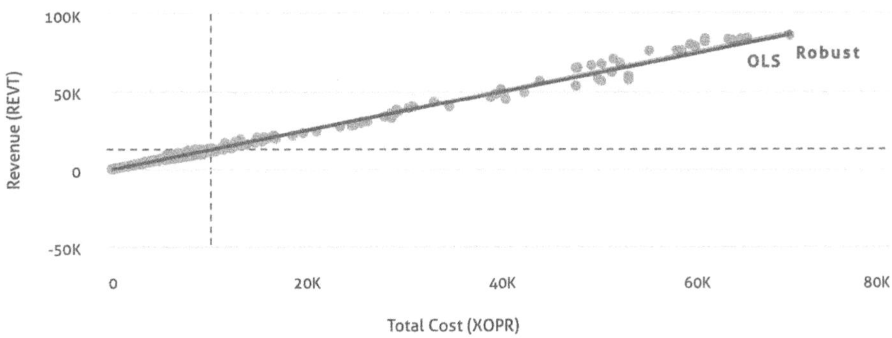

Exhibit 7.8 All companies

Exhibit 7.9 Regression summary ($REVT = \lambda_0 + \lambda_1\, XOPR + \lambda_2\, PPI$)

GVKEY	Companies	Year range	Count	λ_0	λ_1	t-Stat (λ_1)	$\underline{R}^2$
001209	Air Products and Chemicals Inc.	1950–2024	75	Y	1.12	11.0	0.993
001794	Ashland Inc.	19,502,024	75	N	1.03	117.4	0.997
004060	DuPont De Nemours Inc.	1950–2024	75	N	1.13	35.8	0.996
162,401	Huntsman Corp	2002–2024	23	Y	1.14	78.8	0.991
162,129	Mosaic Company (The)	2002–2024	23	N	1.71	9.0	0.958
008247	PPG Industries Inc.	1952–2024	73	N	1.09	20.5	0.999
008762	Procter & Gamble Co (The)	1952–2024	73	N	1.33	27.5	0.997
	All companies	*1950–2024*	*417*	*Y*	*1.27*	*43.0*	*0.993*

Chapter 8
Petroleum Refining

Petroleum refining is the downstream segment of the oil and gas industry. This chapter examines seven corporations engaged in large-scale petroleum refining: Chevron, CVR Energy, ExxonMobil, HF Sinclair, Par Pacific Holdings, Trecora Resources, and Valero Energy.

These corporations process crude oil into end-use products such as gasoline, diesel, jet fuel, and petrochemicals. Their operations constitute the final transformation stage before commercial distribution. Two of the corporations, Chevron and ExxonMobil, are vertically integrated; they operate across exploration, production, refining, and retail channels. The remaining five are focused refiners. Integration status materially influences long-run profitability.

8.1 Regression Analysis

I apply the regression model (Eq. 1.2) to estimate each corporation's operating profit markup. The slope coefficient λ_1 quantifies the markup before depreciation and amortization. A stable λ_1 over time indicates persistent profitability driven by structural cost behavior.

All regressions are robust. The R^2 values exceed 0.983, confirming the explanatory power of XOPR in estimating revenue. This predictive relationship is consistent across corporations with different scales, integration, and geographic reach.

E. A. Silva, *U.S. Corporate Profits, 1950–2024*, SpringerBriefs in Economics,
https://doi.org/10.1007/978-3-032-11399-3_8

8.2 Intercepts and Cost Structure

The regression intercepts vary. Par Pacific Holdings shows a statistically significant intercept, while the remaining corporations report insignificant intercepts. A significant intercept indicates a fixed component of revenue not accounted for by proportional cost scaling. Most refiners operate under conditions where revenue aligns directly with operating costs, supporting the use of λ_1 as the primary metric.

8.3 Two Groups of Slope Coefficients

The slope coefficients divide the seven corporations into two groups: the integrated refiners (Chevron and ExxonMobil) and nonintegrated refiners (CVR Energy, HF Sinclair, Par Pacific Holdings, Trecora Resources, and Valero Energy).

The λ_1 values show the advantages of integration. Chevron and ExxonMobil maintain higher markups than their nonintegrated competitors.

8.4 Regression Results

The regressions exhibit a strong statistical fit. The slope t-statistics are high across the board. These values confirm the reliability of λ_1 and its consistency over time.

There is no evidence of slope convergence. The markups remain corporation specific. Chevron and ExxonMobil do not trend toward the levels observed in smaller, focused refiners. The absence of slope alignment refutes the notion that market competition erodes markup differentials over long periods.

Exhibit 8.9 summarizes the regression results for the representative refining corporations, detailing intercept significance, slope coefficients (λ_1), t-statistics, and R^2 values and illustrating the structural cost dynamics of the industry.

8.5 Summary and Observations

Refining is a depreciable asset-intensive process. Equipment utilization, feedstock selection, and distribution efficiency affect profitability. Larger corporations possess internal infrastructure that buffers supply volatility and improves throughput planning. The industry's profit behavior is structural. Integration, scale, and process control define the markup range. The regression model captures this behavior. The regressions confirm that Total Cost is a sufficient predictor of revenue over long horizons.

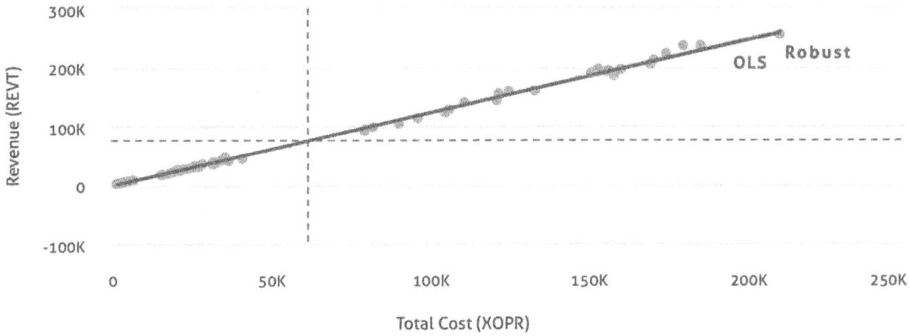

Exhibit 8.1 Chevron Corp

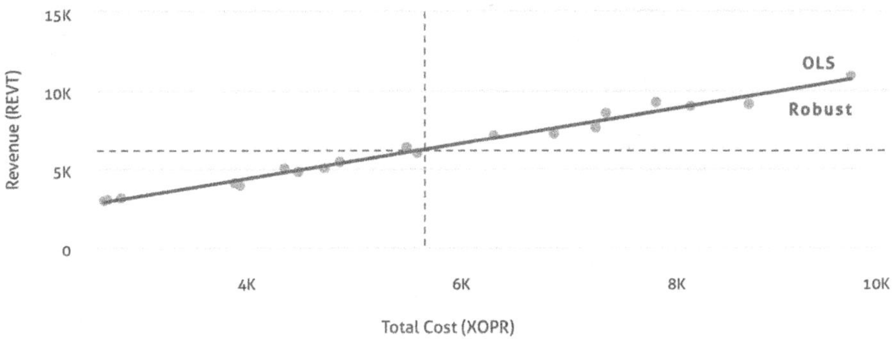

Exhibit 8.2 CVR Energy Inc.

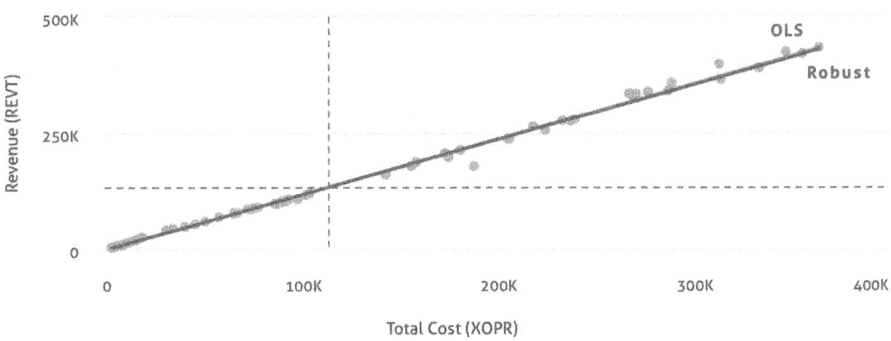

Exhibit 8.3 Exxon Mobil Corp

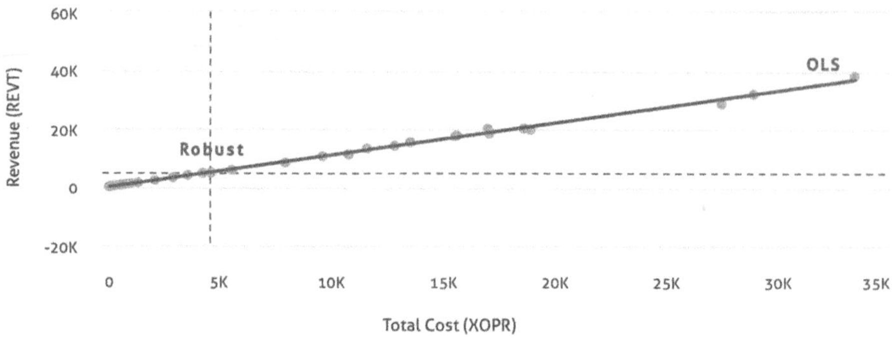

Exhibit 8.4 HF Sinclair Corp

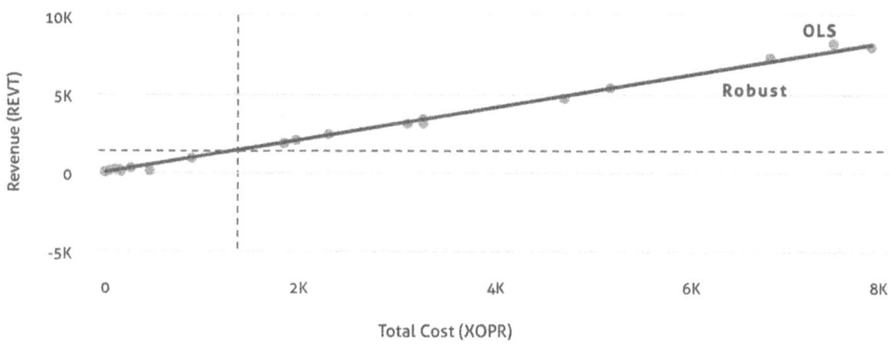

Exhibit 8.5 Par Pacific Holdings Inc.

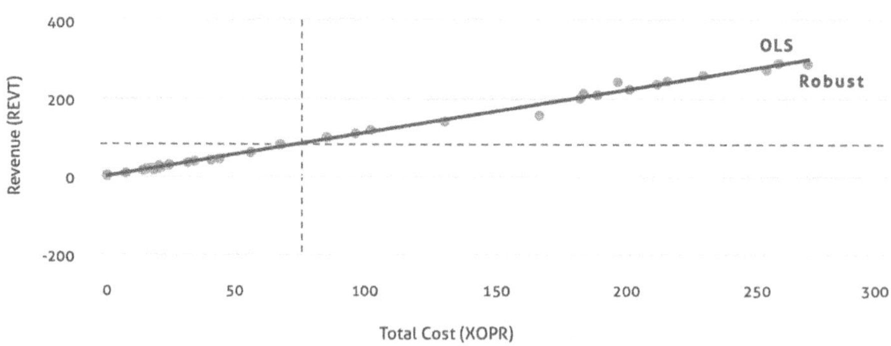

Exhibit 8.6 Trecora Resources

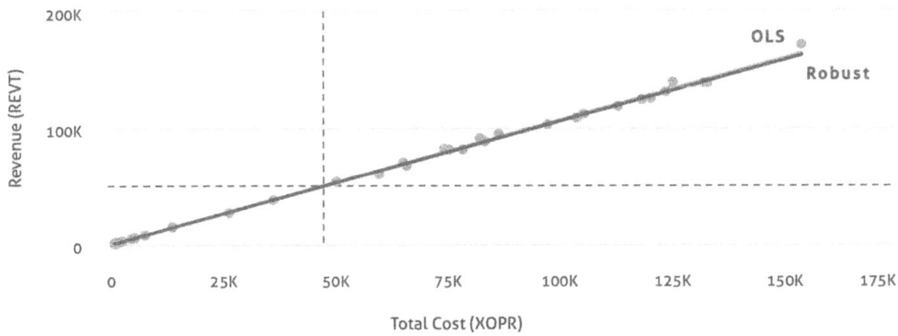

Exhibit 8.7 Valero Energy Corp

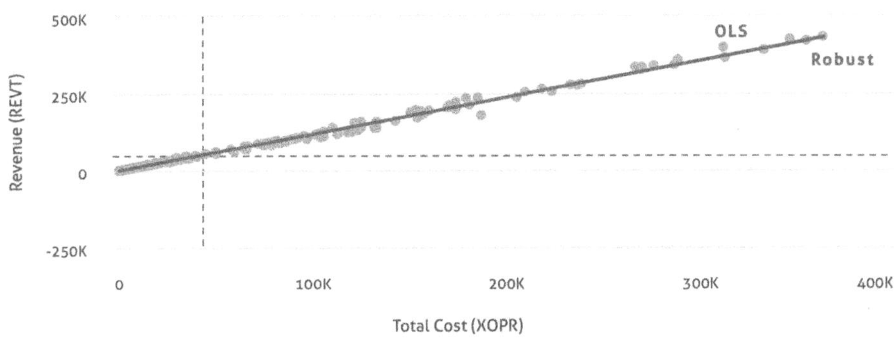

Exhibit 8.8 All companies

Exhibit 8.9 Regression summary ($REVT = \lambda_0 + \lambda_1\, XOPR + \lambda_2\, PPI$)

GVKEY	Companies	Year range	Count	λ_0	λ_1	t-Stat (λ_1)	R^2
002991	Chevron Corp	1960–2024	65	N	1.22	43.2	0.998
178,672	CVR Energy Inc.	2006–2024	19	N	1.10	23.8	0.983
004503	Exxon Mobil Corp	1950–2024	75	N	1.25	33.8	0.997
005667	HF Sinclair Corp	1960–2024	64	N	1.11	77.5	0.998
022447	Par Pacific Holdings Inc.	1988–2024	36	Y	1.08	65.2	0.997
001712	Trecora Resources	1976–2021	46	N	1.13	46.5	0.997
015247	Valero Energy Corp	1979–2024	46	N	1.05	43.9	0.999
	All companies	*1950–2024*	*351*	*N*	*1.196*	*113.7*	*0.996*

Chapter 9
Machinery and Equipment

This chapter examines four legacy corporations in the machinery and equipment industry: Caterpillar, Clark Equipment, Cummins, and Deere & Co. These corporations occupy critical positions in the US industrial landscape. Their product lines include tractors, engines, construction equipment, and mechanical systems used across infrastructure, agriculture, and logistics.

The four corporations maintain long operational histories. Caterpillar, Cummins, and Deere & Co. report annual data over 75 years. Clark Equipment presents a shorter time series.

9.1 Regression Analysis

I apply the reduced-form regression model (Eq. 1.2) to estimate the operating profit markup by regressing REVT on XOPR. The slope coefficient λ_1 reflects the long-run markup before depreciation and amortization. All regressions return strong fits. $\underline{R}^2$ values exceed 0.995 for all four corporations. The regression lines are stable, with minimal OLS estimation divergence.

9.2 Slope Coefficients

The slope coefficients fall within a broad range. Similar to other industries covered in this book, these values reflect sustained profitability over extended business cycles and a lack of profit convergence. These corporations operate in global markets where demand fluctuates with commodity cycles and infrastructure spending. Maintaining markup stability under variable conditions confirms robust cost control and strong market positions.

E. A. Silva, *U.S. Corporate Profits, 1950–2024*, SpringerBriefs in Economics,
https://doi.org/10.1007/978-3-032-11399-3_9

Cummins reports a lower markup than Caterpillar and Deere & Co. Cummins corporation's narrower product specialization, engines and power systems, may constrain pricing flexibility but still supports a stable markup.

9.3 Intercepts and Cost Structures

The intercepts are significant for Clark Equipment, Cummins, and Deere & Co. This indicates fixed components in their cost-revenue relationship. Caterpillar does not display a significant intercept. Its revenue scales proportionally with cost, suggesting limited fixed displacement.

9.4 Regression Results

Each regression exhibits high explanatory power. Deere & Co. ($\underline{R}^2$ = 0.995), Cummins ($\underline{R}^2$= 1.000), and Caterpillar ($\underline{R}^2$= 0.997) confirm the predictive validity of XOPR in estimating revenue. The regression results align with patterns established in previous chapters.

There is no evidence of convergence of the estimated slope coefficients: λ_1 values remain stable and corporation specific. The machinery and equipment industry exhibits differentiated markup patterns that reflect operational scale and product range.

Exhibit 9.6 summarizes the regression outcomes for the representative corporations in this sector, including intercept significance, slope coefficients (λ_1), t-statistics, and R^2 values.

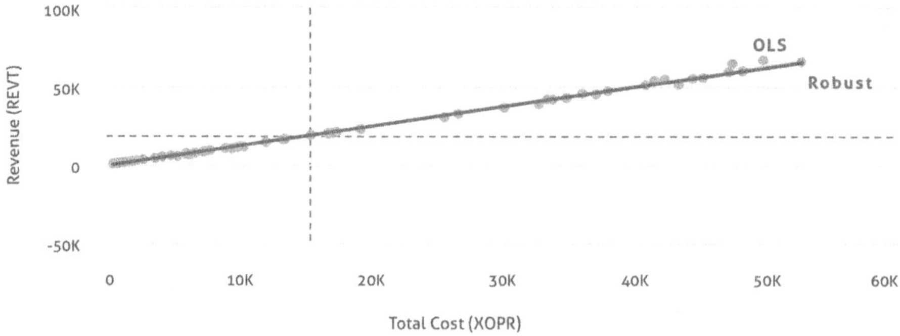

Exhibit 9.1 Caterpillar Inc.

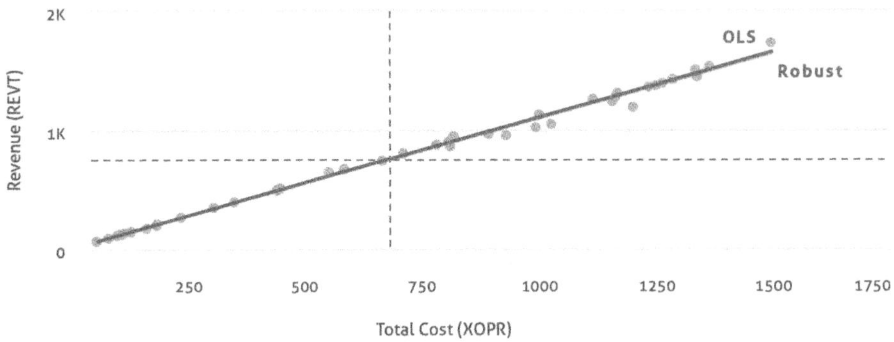

Exhibit 9.2 Clark Equipment Co

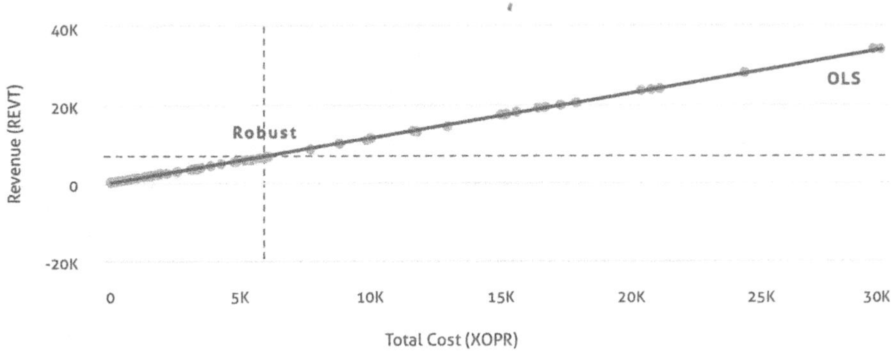

Exhibit 9.3 Cummins Inc.

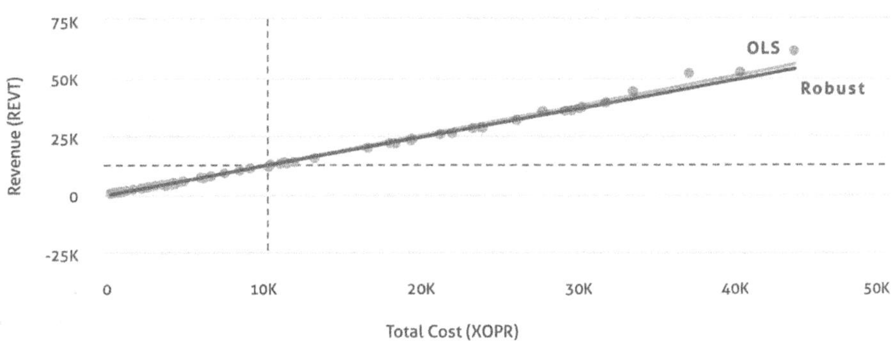

Exhibit 9.4 Deere & Company

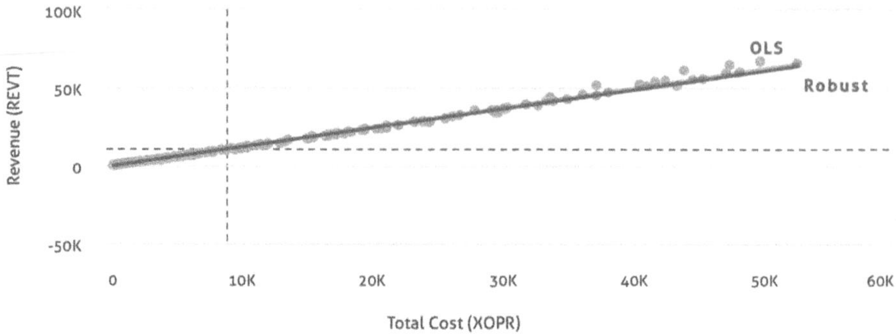

Exhibit 9.5 All companies

Exhibit 9.6: Regression summary ($REVT = \lambda_0 + \lambda_1 XOPR + \lambda_2 PPI$)

GVKEY	Companies	Year range	Count	λ_0	λ_1	t-Stat (λ_1)	$\underline{R}^2$
002817	Caterpillar Inc.	1950–2024	75	N	1.30	37.2	0.997
003091	Clark Equipment Co	1950–1994	45	Y	1.13	44.7	0.996
003650	Cummins Inc.	1950–2024	75	Y	1.19	140.9	1.000
003835	Deere & Company	1950–2024	75	Y	1.43	18.9	0.995
	All companies	*1950–2024*	*270*	*N*	*1.31*	*53.2*	*0.996*

Chapter 10
Computer Equipment and Electronic Devices

This chapter examines eight corporations in the computer equipment and electronic devices sector: AMD, Apple, Applied Materials, Cisco, HP, Intel, Nvidia, and Xilinx. These corporations operate across microprocessor design, semiconductor fabrication, computing infrastructure, and specialized hardware components. Their products form the base layer for modern digital systems, ranging from consumer electronics to data centers, and artificial intelligence.

10.1 Regression Analysis

I apply the adopted the reduced-form regression model (Eq. 1.2) to estimate the operating profit markup before depreciation and amortization. The model yields high $\underline{R}^2$ values across the sample.

10.2 Slope Coefficients and Markup Range

The slope coefficients vary, with HP at the floor and Nvidia at the ceiling, followed by Intel and Applied Materials. The midrange includes AMD, Cisco, and Xilinx.

Slope *t*-statistics exceed 9.4, confirming the robustness of markup estimates. The markup dispersion may reflect product specialization and market positioning (number of corporations in the industry offering similar products and services).

E. A. Silva, *U.S. Corporate Profits, 1950–2024*, SpringerBriefs in Economics, https://doi.org/10.1007/978-3-032-11399-3_10

10.3 Intercepts

Intercepts vary across corporations. AMD, Applied Materials, Nvidia, and Xilinx report significant intercepts. These intercepts indicate structural revenue not accounted for by proportional cost behavior. A significant intercept affects the interpretation of profit ratios and supports regression-based profit markup as the correct measure of performance.

Apple, Cisco, HP, and Intel exhibit nonsignificant intercepts, which implies that cost structures drive revenue generation. In these cases, cost scaling accounts for nearly all variance in revenue.

10.4 Regression Results

The regressions exhibit high explanatory power. $\underline{R}^2$ values exceed 0.990 in six of the eight corporations. Due to recent growth acceleration, the lowest $\underline{R}^2$ belongs to Nvidia ($\underline{R}^2 = 0.947$). This recent performance includes a revenue surge from 2023 to 2024, where Nvidia's reported revenue more than doubled in 2 years.[1]

These results do not alter the core conclusion: the regression model (Eq. 1.2) provides a reliable linear fit across the industry. The slope coefficient λ_1 remains the primary metric of long-run operating profits performance.

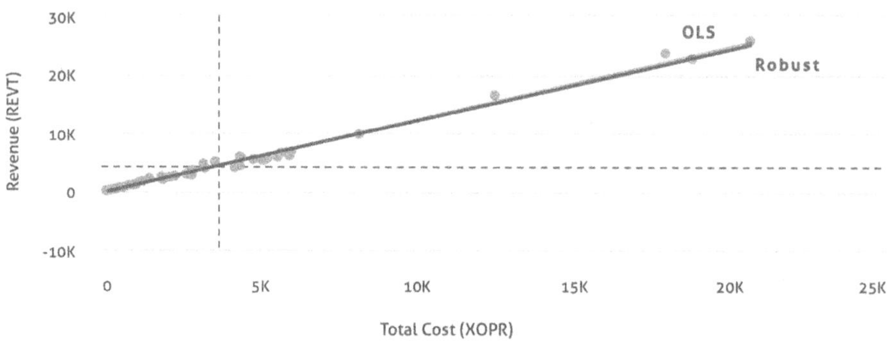

Exhibit 10.1 AMD

[1] Nvidia has a short history compared to the other companies in the sample, and it shows an extraordinary operating profit markup that is unlikely to endure in the future.

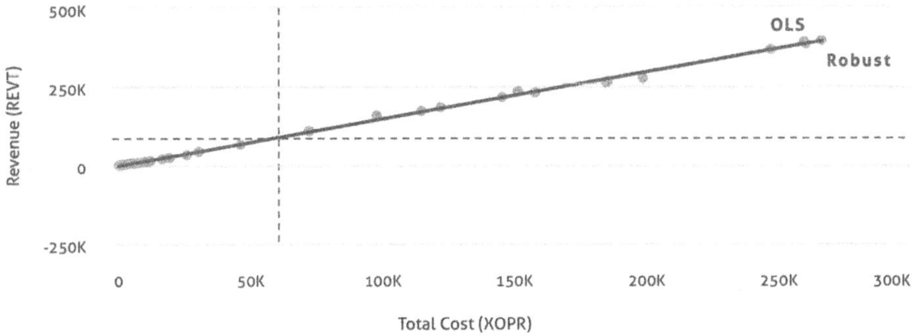

Exhibit 10.2 Apple

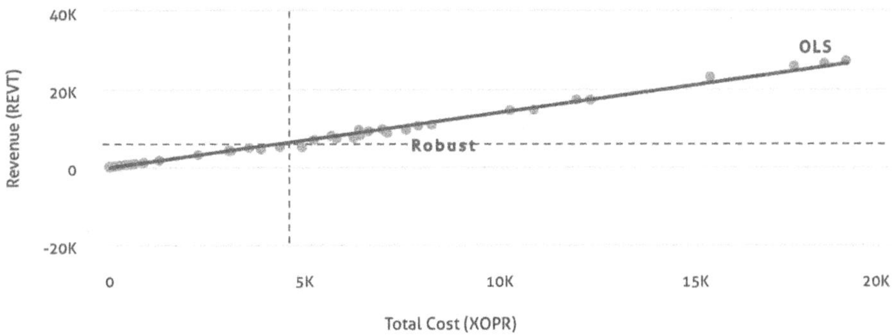

Exhibit 10.3 Applied Materials

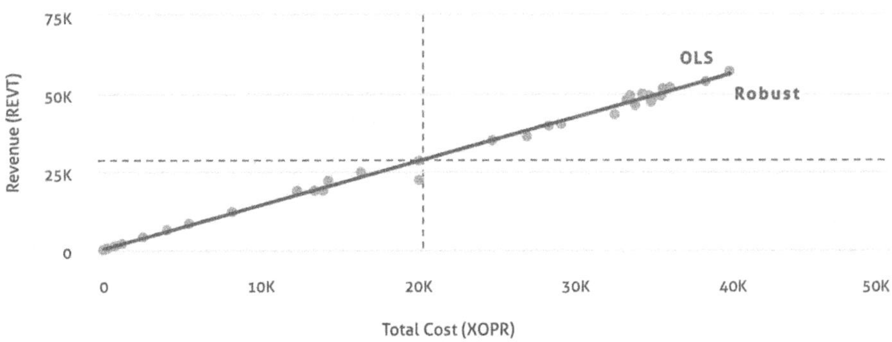

Exhibit 10.4 Cisco

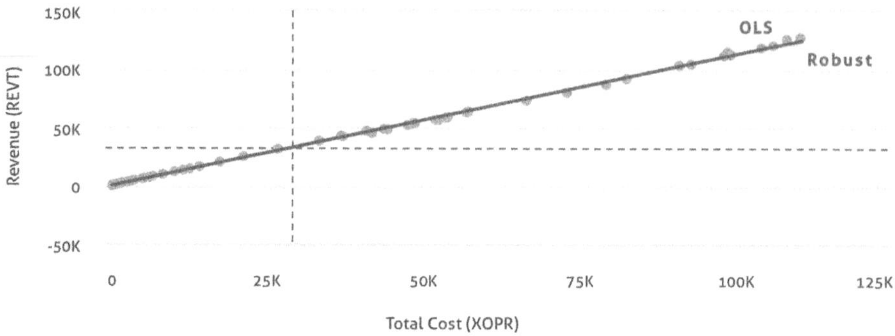

Exhibit 10.5 HP

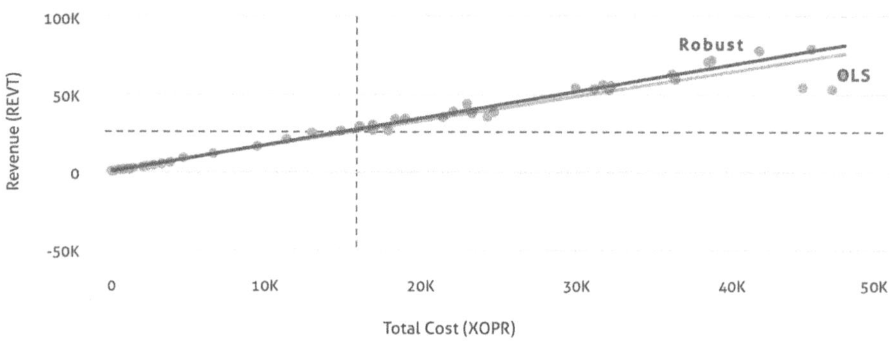

Exhibit 10.6 Intel

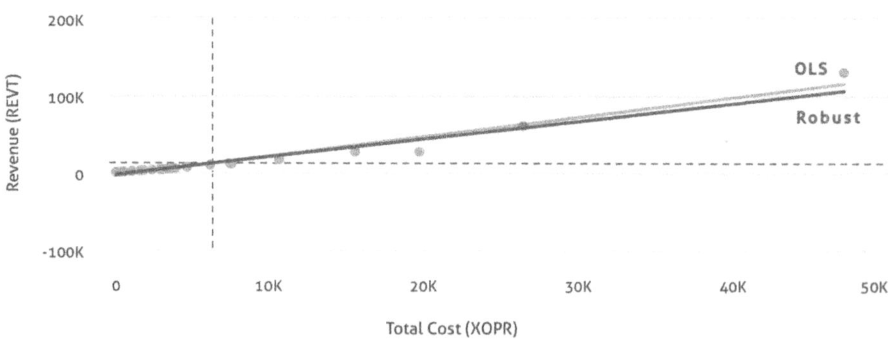

Exhibit 10.7 Nvidia

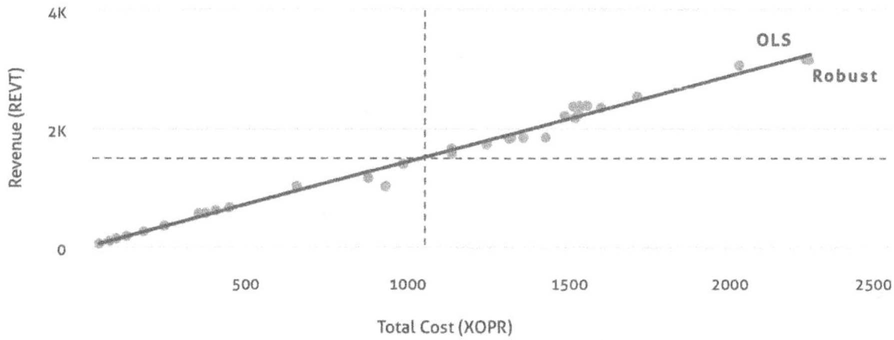

Exhibit 10.8 Xilinx

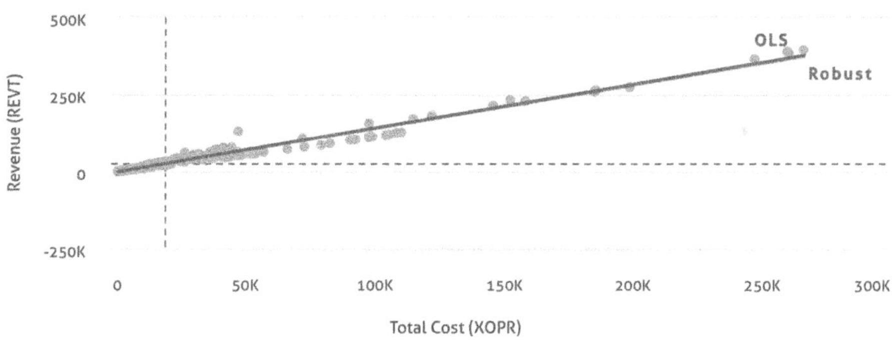

Exhibit 10.9 All companies

Exhibit 10.10 Regression summary ($REVT = \lambda_0 + \lambda_1\ XOPR + \lambda_2\ PPI$)

GVKEY	Companies	Year range	Count	λ_0	λ_1	t-Stat (λ_1)	R^2
001161	Advanced Micro Devices Inc.	1972–2024	53	Y	1.35	37.5	0.993
001690	Apple Inc.	1980–2024	45	N	1.47	46.7	0.999
001704	Applied Materials Inc.	1972–2024	53	Y	1.58	30.5	0.996
020779	Cisco Systems Inc.	1989–2022	36	N	1.30	21.2	0.995
005606	HP Inc.	1952–2024	73	N	1.14	69.9	0.999
006008	Intel Corp	1971–2024	54	N	1.86	9.4	0.999
117,768	Nvidia Corporation	1996–2024	29	Y	3.0	43.8	0.947
022325	Xilinx Inc.[a]	1989–2020	32	Y	1.27	33.4	0.990
	All companies	*1950–2024*	*375*	*N*	*1.41*	*30.9*	*0.980*

[a]Xilinx was announced to be acquired by AMD in 2020, a process which was fully completed in 2022

Chapter 11
Transportation Equipment

This chapter analyzes eight legacy corporations in the transportation equipment industry: Aerojet Rocketdyne, American Motors, Curtiss-Wright, Dana, Ford Motor, General Motors, Honeywell International, and Navistar International. These corporations include aerospace systems, automotive manufacturing, propulsion, and defense-related equipment. They are long-standing participants in the US industrial base.

The industry shows consistent markup behavior over time. The slope coefficient λ_1 estimates the operating profit markup before depreciation and amortization. $\underline{R}^2$ values exceed 0.99 for all companies, validating the reliability of the regression model (Eq. 1.2) across the sector.

11.1 Slope Coefficients and Long-Run Profitability

The regression slope λ_1 coefficients for this group range from 1.08 to 1.27. Ford Motor is the standout performer in this industry group, boasting the highest long-term operating profit markup, followed by Curtiss-Wright and American Motors. These corporations maintain diversified portfolios that include automobile manufacturing, aerospace, and specialty defense systems.

Navistar International reports the lowest operating profit markup, reflecting sensitivity to cyclical demand in commercial trucking.[1]

[1] Navistar International has become International Motors LLC, since July 2021, a division of the Volkswagen Group.

E. A. Silva, *U.S. Corporate Profits, 1950–2024*, SpringerBriefs in Economics, https://doi.org/10.1007/978-3-032-11399-3_11

11.2 Intercepts

Five of the eight corporations present significant intercepts. The remaining three show nonsignificant intercepts, indicating proportional scaling between cost and revenue. For most companies, the slope coefficient captures cost structure variation.

11.3 Regression Results

Each regression displays a strong fit, with high slope t-statistics. The linear relationship between REVT and XOPR remains stable throughout the period analyzed. There is no evidence of convergence toward a central point among slope coefficients of the corporations in the sample. Differences in the slope λ_1 persist, suggesting that operating profit behavior is corporation specific.

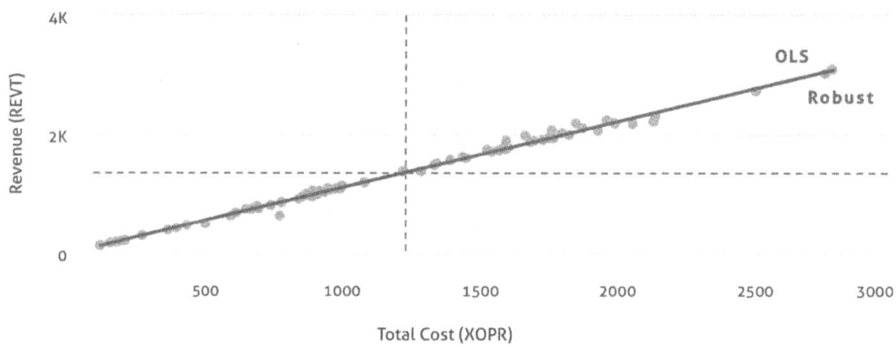

Exhibit 11.1 Aerojet Rocketdyne Holdings Inc.

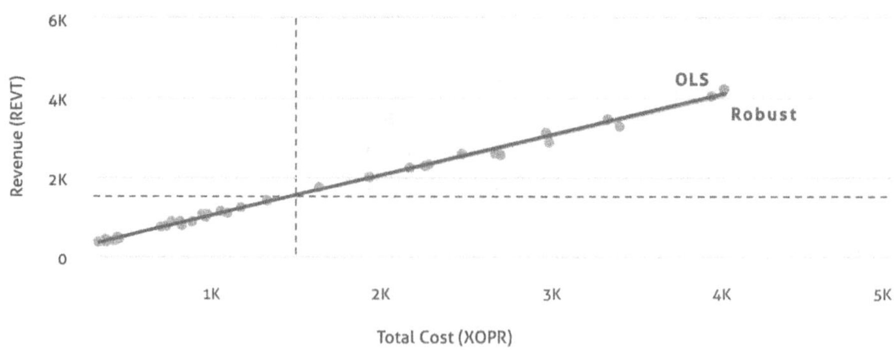

Exhibit 11.2 American Motors Corp

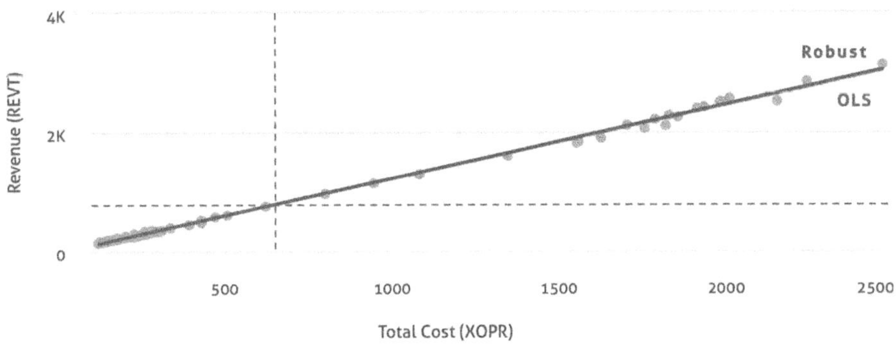

Exhibit 11.3 Curtiss-Wright Corp

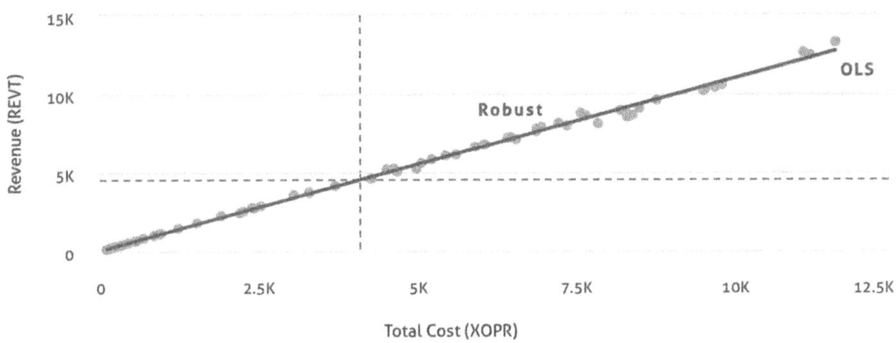

Exhibit 11.4 Dana Inc.

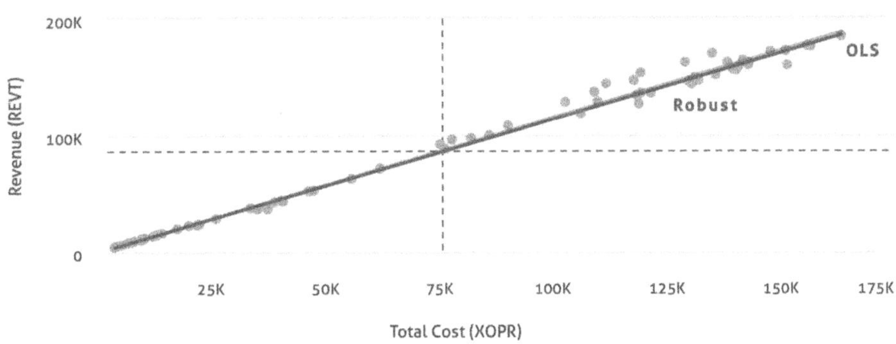

Exhibit 11.5 Ford Motor Co

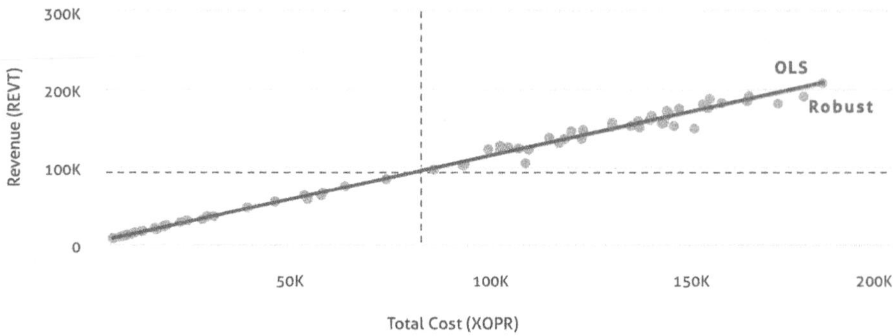

Exhibit 11.6 General Motors Co

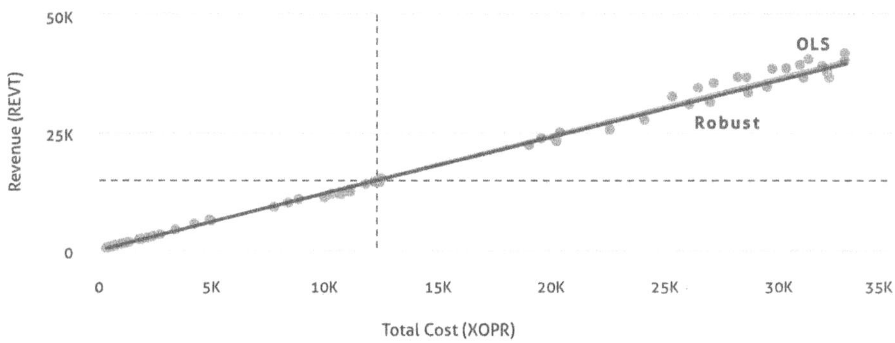

Exhibit 11.7 Honeywell International Inc.

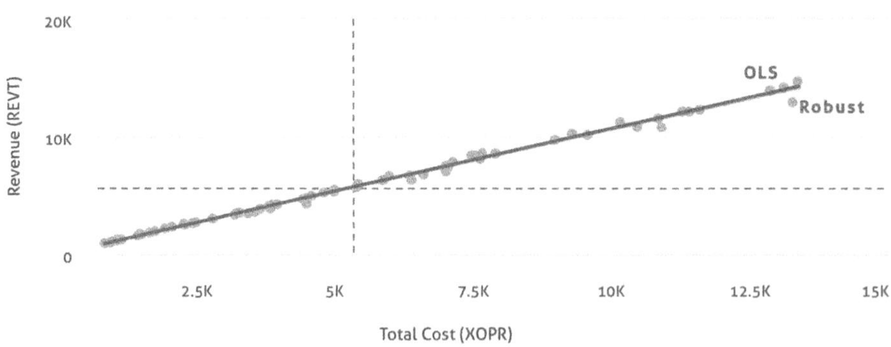

Exhibit 11.8 Navistar International Corp

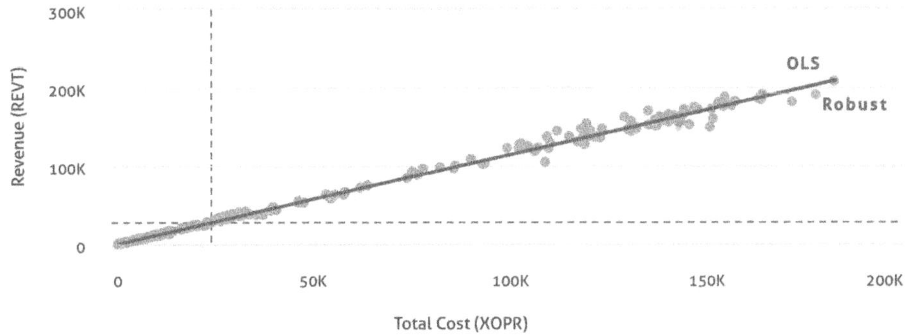

Exhibit 11.9 All companies

Exhibit 11.10 Regression summary ($REVT = \lambda_0 + \lambda_1 XOPR + \lambda_2 PPI$)

GVKEY	Companies	Year range	Count	λ_0	λ_1	t-Stat (λ_1)	$\underline{R}^2$
005018	Aerojet Rocketdyne holdings Inc.	1950–2022	73	N	1.1	67.8	0.994
001517	American motors Corp	1950–2022	37	Y	1.16	27.4	0.997
003662	Curtiss-Wright Corp	1950–2024	75	Y	1.21	60.2	0.998
003734	Dana Inc.	1950–2024	75	Y	1.11	37.3	0.997
004839	Ford motor co	1955–2024	70	Y	1.27	20.7	0.995
005073	General motors co	1950–2024	75	N	1.1	27.5	0.992
001300	Honeywell international Inc.	1950–2024	75	Y	1.13	16.7	0.995
006081	Navistar international Corp	1950–2020	71	N	1.08	51.7	0.995
	All companies	*1950–2024*	*551*	*N*	*1.14*	*91.4*	*0.997*

Chapter 12
Government Contractors

In *The Fiscal Crisis of the State* (1973), James O'Connor divided the US economy into three market segments, identifying oligopolies as dominant in two.[1] These were the competitive sector, not represented in SEC filings, and the oligopoly sector selling to government agencies.

O'Connor posited the testable hypothesis that the workforce in the government contracting sector was better protected and compensated, due to the greater ability of these corporations to pass through payroll costs and expenses. This ability, in turn, preserved the profit markups through amended government contracts that adjusted for budget overruns.

This chapter examines eight corporations that generate substantial revenue from government contracts: Boeing, General Dynamics, L3Harris, Lockheed Martin, Northrop, Raytheon, RTX, and Textron. These corporations operate in defense, aerospace, and advanced systems integration. Their business models rely on long-cycle government procurement, regulated pricing frameworks, and embedded cost recovery structures.

The analysis focuses on long-run profitability using the adopted regression model (Eq. 1.2). The results confirm that government contractors maintain persistent, corporation-specific operating profit markups over time.

[1] James O'Connor, *The Fiscal Crisis of the State* (New York: St. Martin's Press, 1973). I attended his graduate seminar; quantitative tests of the book's hypotheses were absent. The analysis is literary political economy, not model-driven, measurement-oriented economics.

E. A. Silva, *U.S. Corporate Profits, 1950–2024*, SpringerBriefs in Economics,
https://doi.org/10.1007/978-3-032-11399-3_12

12.1 Slope Coefficients and Markup Consistency

The regression slope λ_1 values range from 1.11 to 1.27, with Northrop at the floor and RTX at the ceiling. The long-run operating profit markup of the remaining corporations shows similar magnitudes, varying from 16% to 25%.

12.2 Intercepts and Structural Differences

Five of the eight corporations, General Dynamics, L3Harris, Northrop, RTX, and Textron, present significant intercepts, suggesting a fixed revenue component independent of direct cost scaling. Boeing, Lockheed, and Raytheon exhibit nonsignificant intercepts; their cost structures align more directly with revenue variability.

12.3 Regression Results

The slope t-statistics range from 25.5 (Raytheon) to 111.7 (General Dynamics), confirming the strength of the linear fit. The $\underline{R}^2$ values exceed 0.99 for all corporations, underscoring the explanatory power of XOPR in predicting REVT.

Markup persistence across these corporations suggests that defense contracting allows for cost recovery and profit stability under long-term government budgets.

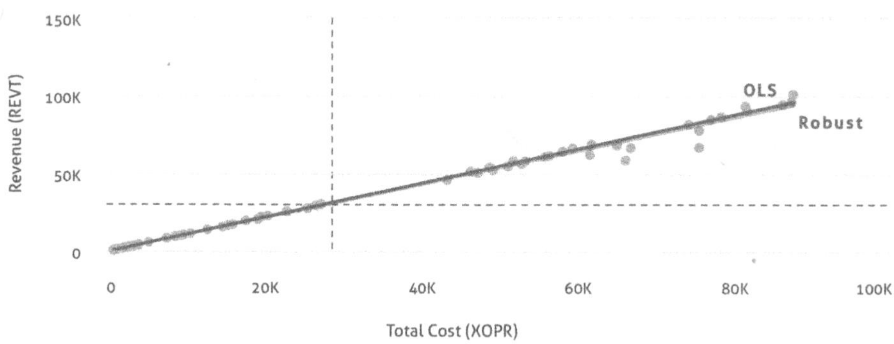

Exhibit 12.1 Boeing Co

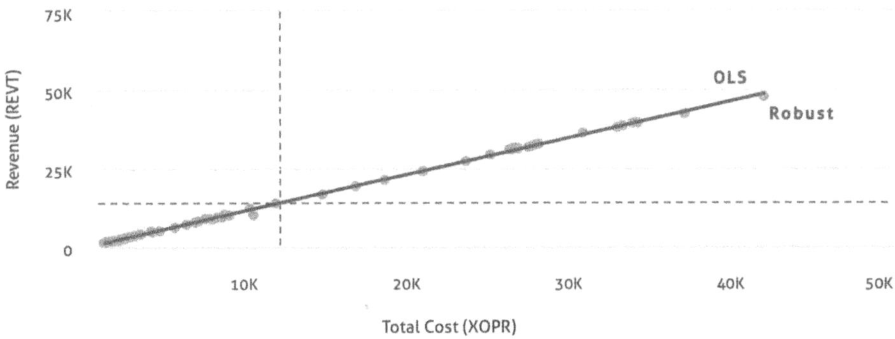

Exhibit 12.2 General Dynamics Corp

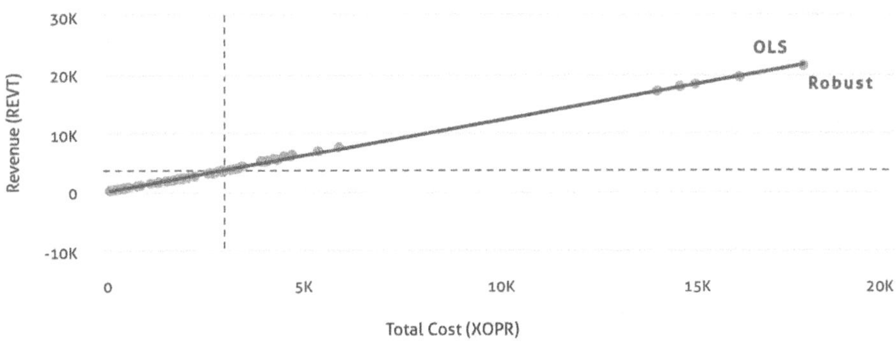

Exhibit 12.3 L3Harris Technologies Inc.

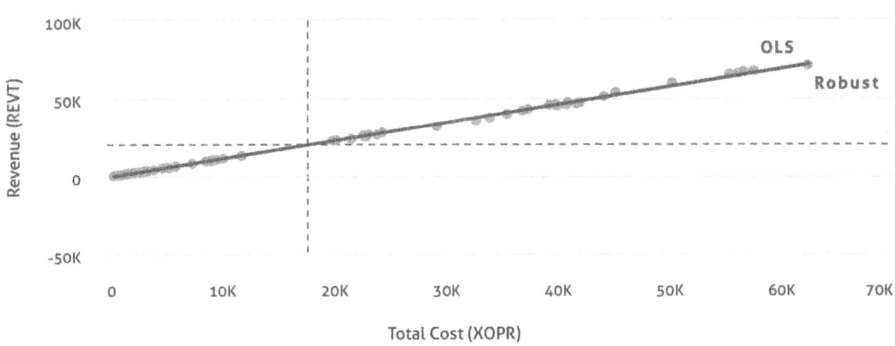

Exhibit 12.4 Lockheed Martin Corp

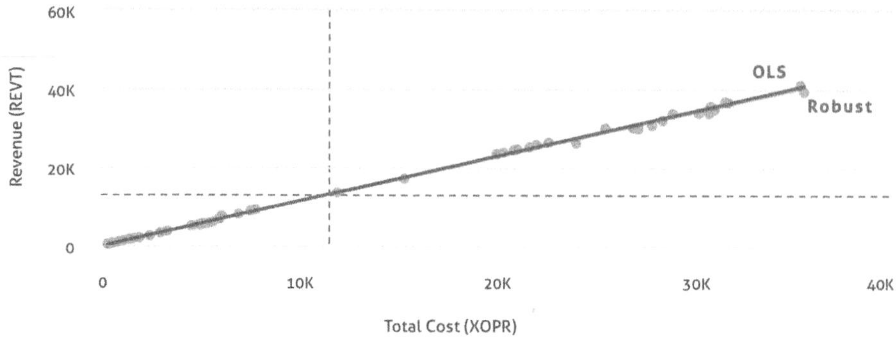

Exhibit 12.5 Northrop Grumman Corp

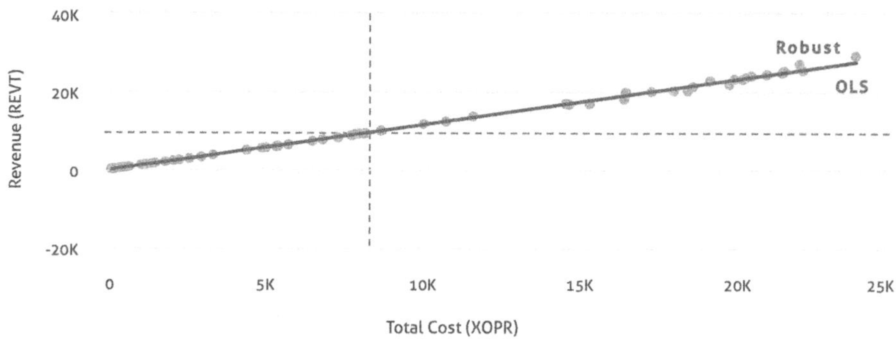

Exhibit 12.6 Raytheon Co.

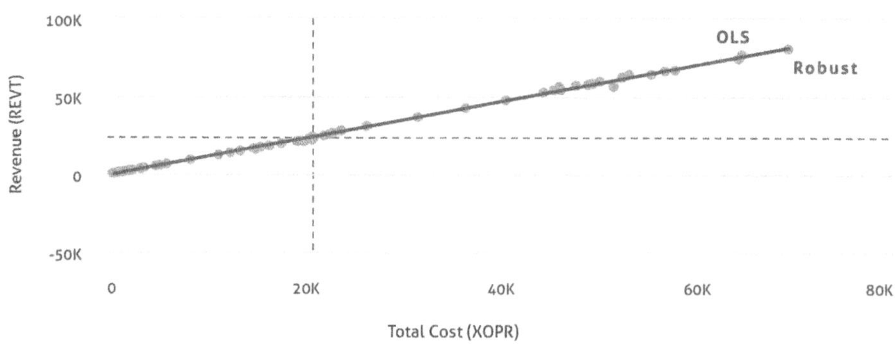

Exhibit 12.7 RTX Corp

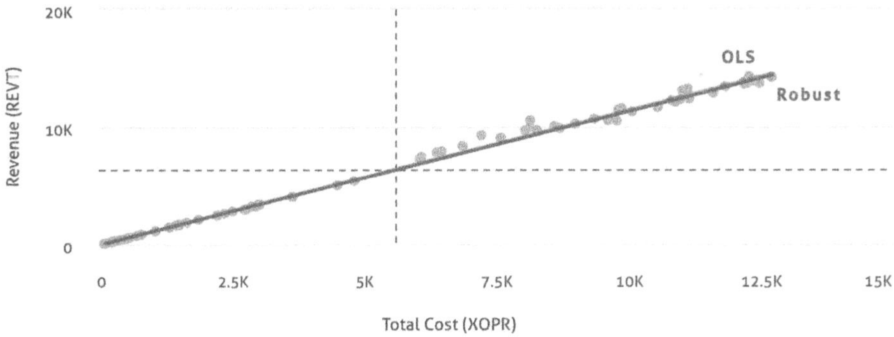

Exhibit 12.8 Textron Inc.

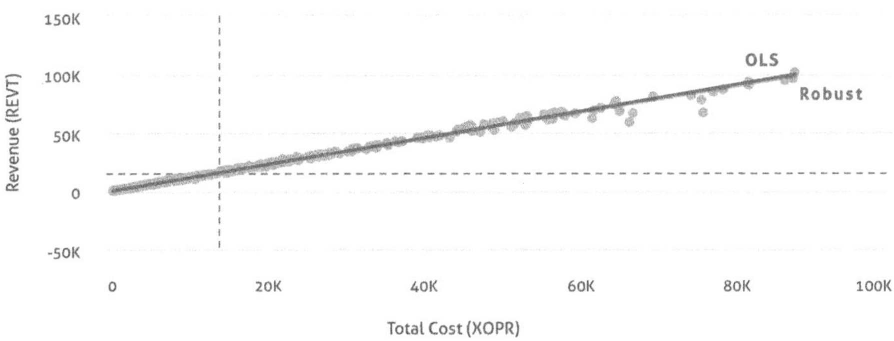

Exhibit 12.9 All companies

Exhibit 12.10 Regression summary (*REVT* = $\lambda_0 + \lambda_1$ *XOPR* + λ_2 *PPI*)

GVKEY	Companies	Year range	Count	λ_0	λ_1	t-Stat (λ_1)	$\underline{R}^2$
002285	Boeing co	1950–2024	75	N	1.17	28	0.993
005046	General Dynamics Corp	1960–2024	65	Y	1.16	111.7	0.999
005492	L3Harris technologies Inc.	1958–2024	67	Y	1.2	97	0.999
006774	Lockheed Martin Corp	1950–2024	75	N	1.18	47.3	0.999
007985	Northrop Grumman Corp	1961–2024	64	Y	1.11	47.9	0.999
008972	Raytheon co.	1950–2019	70	N	1.16	25.5	0.998
010983	RTX Corp	1950–2024	75	Y	1.27	44.7	0.999
010519	Textron Inc.	1950–2024	75	Y	1.25	38.7	0.997
	All companies	*1950–2024*	*566*	*Y*	*1.10*	*63.3*	*0.995*

Chapter 13
Computer Services

The computer services industry includes corporations that emerged during the second wave of high technology following World War II. This evolution followed the initial growth of Fairchild Semiconductor and International Business Machines Corp (IBM)-associated corporations and gave rise to a broad sector encompassing software enterprises, computer networks, and computer-related devices. These corporations supply infrastructure and platform-level services, enabling connectivity, automation, and digital productivity across industries.

The eight corporations examined in this chapter are Adobe, Alphabet, Amazon, Electronic Data Systems Corp (EDS), IBM, Microsoft, Oracle, and Unisys. Although their profiles differ substantially in terms of business model and longevity, all are key participants in the development and scaling of digital infrastructure in the US and global economies.

13.1 Regression Analysis and Profit Behavior

I apply the adopted regression model (Eq. 1.2) to estimate each corporation's long-run operating profit markup. The slope coefficients are stable, with four corporations (Adobe, Alphabet, Microsoft, and Oracle) behaving above the sector average and four corporations (Amazon, EDS, IBM, and Unisys) falling below the sector average.

Intercept significance varies among this group of companies. Several computer corporations display nonsignificant intercepts, while others include a fixed component in their cost-revenue structure. This variation is not anomalous but reflects the diverse structures of corporations that span computer hardware, software, cloud services, and digital consulting.

E. A. Silva, *U.S. Corporate Profits, 1950–2024*, SpringerBriefs in Economics,
https://doi.org/10.1007/978-3-032-11399-3_13

13.2 Adobe, Microsoft, and Oracle's Markup

Adobe, Microsoft, and Oracle present the highest slope coefficients in this chapter and among the highest in the entire dataset. The magnitude of these markups approaches those observed in the pharmaceutical sector, which is notable given the difference in regulation and pricing structures between industries.

Such profit persistence over decades suggests enduring market power rooted in proprietary software ecosystems and high switching costs. These levels of high operating profit markup cannot persist without government collusion. The complex interaction between oligopoly structures and captured regulatory accommodation is a subject beyond the scope of this book.

13.3 Amazon, EDS, and Unisys' Markup

Amazon, EDS, and Unisys report the lowest slope coefficients within the group. Despite its massive scale and rapid expansion, Amazon's low slope coefficient reflects its cost-intensive business model and reinvestment strategy. EDS and Unisys show similar margin constraints.

13.4 Intercepts

Intercepts are significant for Adobe, Amazon, and Unisys. These results indicate a baseline component of revenue unrelated to directly scaled costs. Such fixed displacement often reflects long-term contracts, licensing fees, or platform maintenance revenues that persist regardless of invoiced volumes.

Alphabet, EDS, IBM, Microsoft, and Oracle show statistically insignificant intercepts. In these cases, revenues scale proportionally with operating costs.

13.5 Regression Results

All eight corporate regressions report high $\underline{R}^2$values, ranging from 0.981 (Microsoft) to 0.998 (Amazon). The regression results confirm that XOPR is a reliable predictor of REVT across decades of financial reporting. The slope coefficients remain corporation specific and time invariant, validating the use of the adopted regression model (Eq. 1.2) for long-run profit analysis.

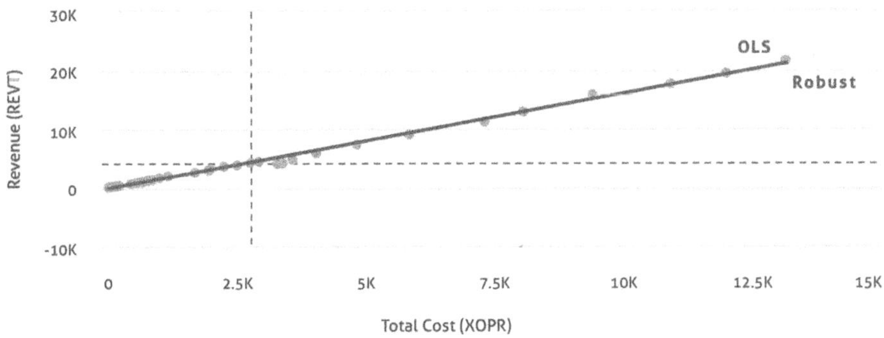

Exhibit 13.1 Adobe Inc.

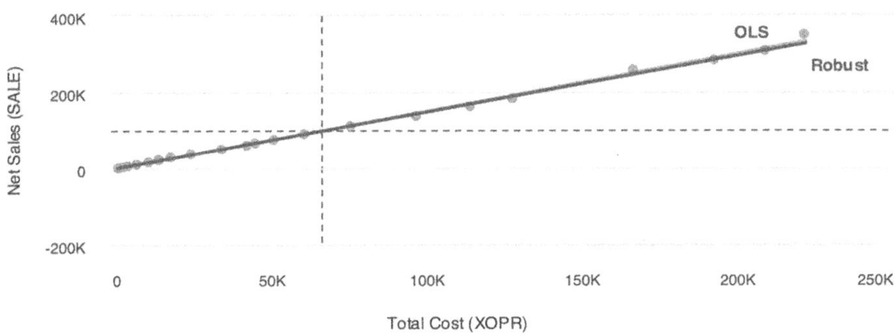

Exhibit 13.2 Alphabet Inc.

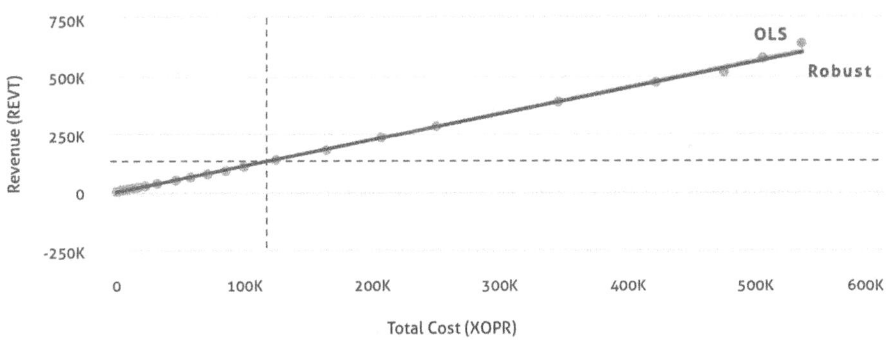

Exhibit 13.3 Amazon.com Inc.

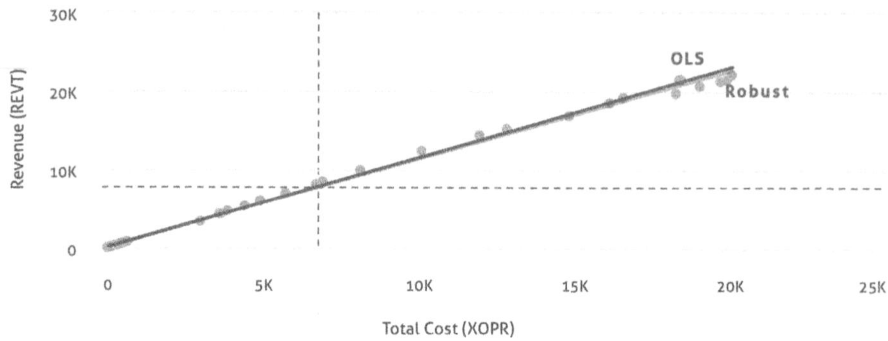

Exhibit 13.4 Electronic Data Systems Corp

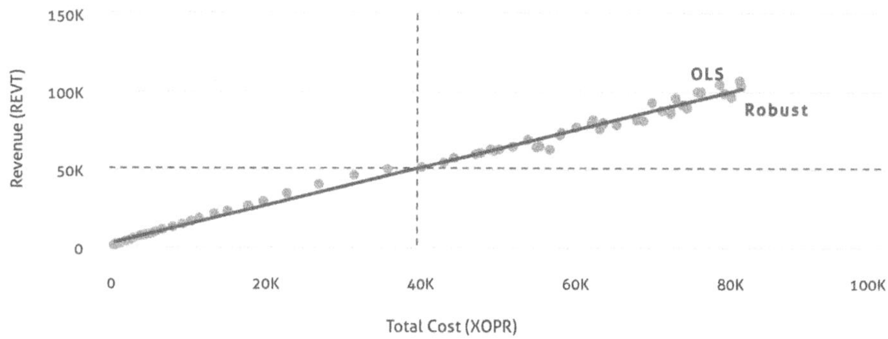

Exhibit 13.5 International Business Machines Corp

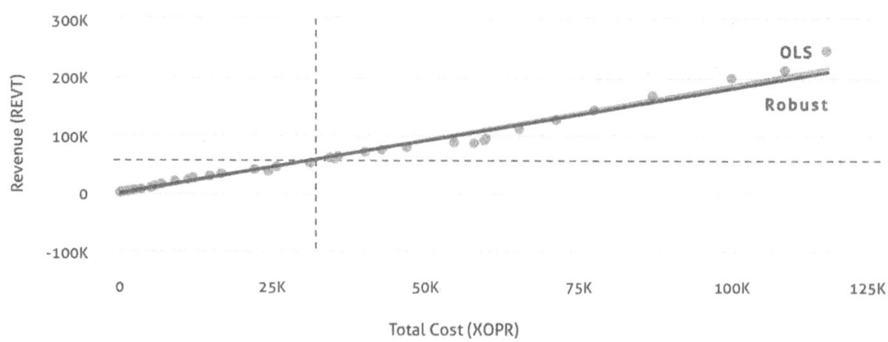

Exhibit 13.6 Microsoft Corp

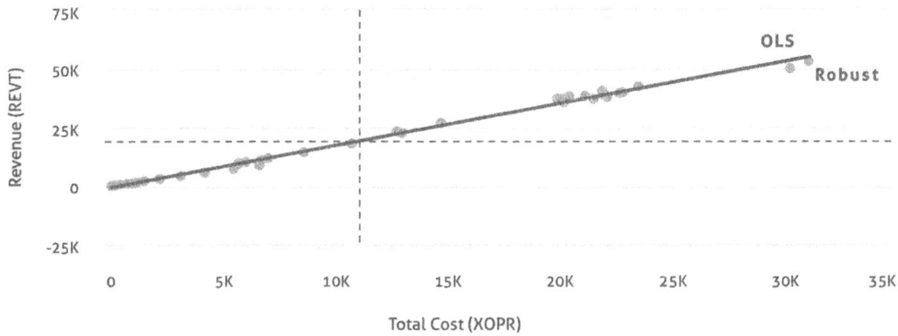

Exhibit 13.7 Oracle Corp

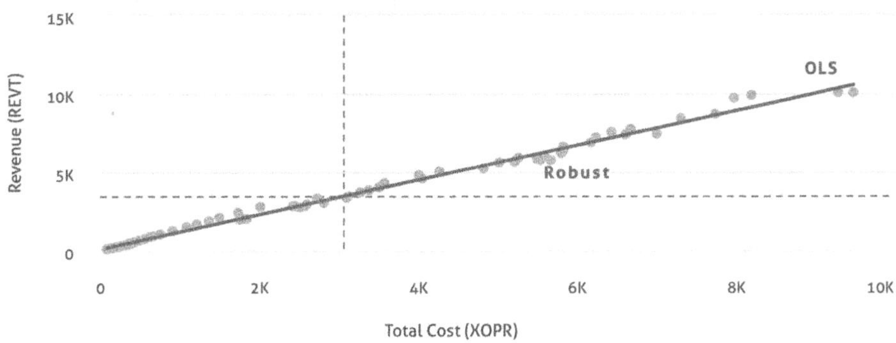

Exhibit 13.8 Unisys Corp

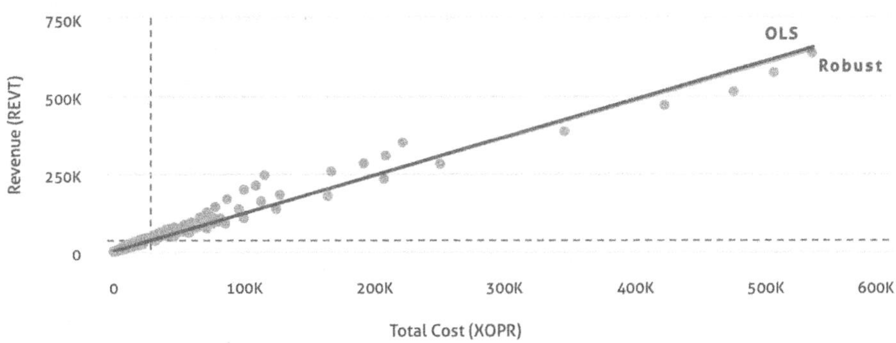

Exhibit 13.9 All companies

Exhibit 13.10 Regression summary (*REVT* = $\lambda_0 + \lambda_1$ *XOPR* + λ_2 *PPI*)

GVKEY	Company[a]	Year range	Count	λ_0	λ_1	*t*-Stat (λ_1)	$\underline{R}^2$
012540	Adobe Inc.	1985–2024	40	Y	1.73	33.3	0.997
160,329	Alphabet Inc.	2002–2024	23	N	1.49	40.4	0.997
064768	Amazon.com Inc.	1995–2024	30	Y	1.15	59.5	0.998
005074	Electronic Data Systems Corp[b]	1968–2007	40	N	1.11	43.5	0.997
006066	International Business Machines Corp	1956–2024	69	N	1.16	27.8	0.994
012141	Microsoft Corp	1985–2024	40	N	2.09	9.9	0.981
012142	Oracle Corp	1985–2024	40	N	1.76	14.9	0.995
002504	Unisys Corp	1950–2024	75	Y	1.11	88.1	0.993
	All companies	*1950–2024*	*357*	*Y*	*1.17*	*22.4*	*0.973*

[a]Meta was initially part of this selection, but given the small number of observations and the fact that its markup is an outlier, it was removed from this text to avoid distortion of the long-run industry data

[b]Electronic Data Systems (EDS) was acquired by HP in 2008

Chapter 14
Book Summary

This chapter presents the overall results of the regression analysis conducted across 71 major US corporations from 1950 to 2024. The analysis used the reduced-form regression model (Eq. 1.2) to estimate the slope coefficient λ_1, which reflects the long-run operating profit markup before depreciation and amortization. The data cover 11 distinct industries, including petroleum, manufacturing, pharmaceuticals, chemicals, computing, defense contracting, and services.

14.1 Limitations of Prior Literature

The existing economics literature on *corporate operating profits* is sparse. Dennis Mueller and his collaborators used models employing a different dependent variable and lacked economic structure. These models treat corporate net (not operating) profits divided by total assets as an autoregressive time series, abstracting away cost structures and enterprise behavior. As a result, they fail to provide a theoretical or structural explanation for profit markup persistence.

Books created by accounting experts and business schools pundits often focus on ratio analysis, frequently relying on net income (net profit) or "earnings" that include passive income, after interest deductions. These methods do not incorporate structural economic modeling and usually ignore operating profits.

14.2 Structural Modeling of Profits

In contrast to these sparse prior approaches, this book adopts a structural economic framework that views corporate profits as the outcome of two integrated processes represented by two simple equations. The first equation is an accounting identity,

E. A. Silva, *U.S. Corporate Profits, 1950–2024*, SpringerBriefs in Economics,
https://doi.org/10.1007/978-3-032-11399-3_14

which is true by definition: REVT = XOPR + OIBDP. The second equation is a testable behavioral equation: OIBDP = f(XOPR) + error.

These two equations are combined to create a reduced-form regression model (Eq. 1.2), allowing direct estimation of the slope coefficient λ_1, the long-term operating profit markup, and the indirect least-squares measurement of the operating profit margin.

I have not imposed linearity in the structural equation. Instead, I explored the coordinate pairs XOPR and REVT by scatterplots using a nonparametric local regression (Loess) scout and discovered, as an empirical result and not a presumption (or à priori specification), that the linear regression, *including an intercept*, provides good data fit to the reduced-form equation. My specification searches leading to the usual linear regression fit should not discourage others from data exploration using the Loess scout.

My approach distinguishes between ratio-based descriptions and economically interpretable regression coefficients, offering a more robust and theoretically grounded understanding of corporate operating profit behavior.

14.3 Principal Findings

Several key results emerge from this structural and data-driven approach. Ratio analysis is ineffective. Operating profit ratios, as used in conventional financial reporting and business textbooks, lack explanatory power. They are descriptive (not predictive) and dissociate from economic theory. In contrast, the regression slope λ_1 offers a testable, interpretable metric of corporate operating profit behavior grounded in enterprise cost structure.

The linear profit equation (1.2) is resilient across industries and 74 years of history. As specified, the structural linear model yields high explanatory power. The $\underline{R}^2$ values across all industries and corporations are consistently high, often exceeding 0.99. These robust $\underline{R}^2$ values indicate that XOPR is a reliable and stable predictor of REVT over long time horizons, with the slope coefficient measuring the operating profit markup.

Intercepts vary across corporations. While slope coefficients are stable, intercepts vary in magnitude (measured in the same monetary units as REVT and XOPR) and significance. Some corporations show a statistically significant intercept, implying a fixed revenue component independent of variable cost; others do not. This variation reflects differences in embedded less variable, fixed, or inflexible costs.

This book's central empirical finding is that the slope λ_1 remains stable and is corporation specific over decades. There is no evidence of the markup convergence across corporations or within industries. Contrary to standard economic claims that suggest competitive equalization of profits (however scaled), the data show that oligopolistic structures enable persistent operating profit markup advantages or the concomitant ability to pass through cost increases to customers. Hence, cost-saving technical innovations have not produced deflation.[1]

In the singular case of Occidental Petroleum, a power function transformation was used to better capture the nonlinearities observed in the data. Even in that case, the long-run behavior of profits remained consistent with the overall findings.

This is my corporate profits book thesis: Oligopolies can maintain high and stable operating profit markups across business cycles. My auxiliary thesis: Oligopolies and the associated barriers to entry prevent profit markup convergence across industries. I demonstrate by the preponderance of evidence the first thesis and provide circumstantial evidence to support the second thesis.

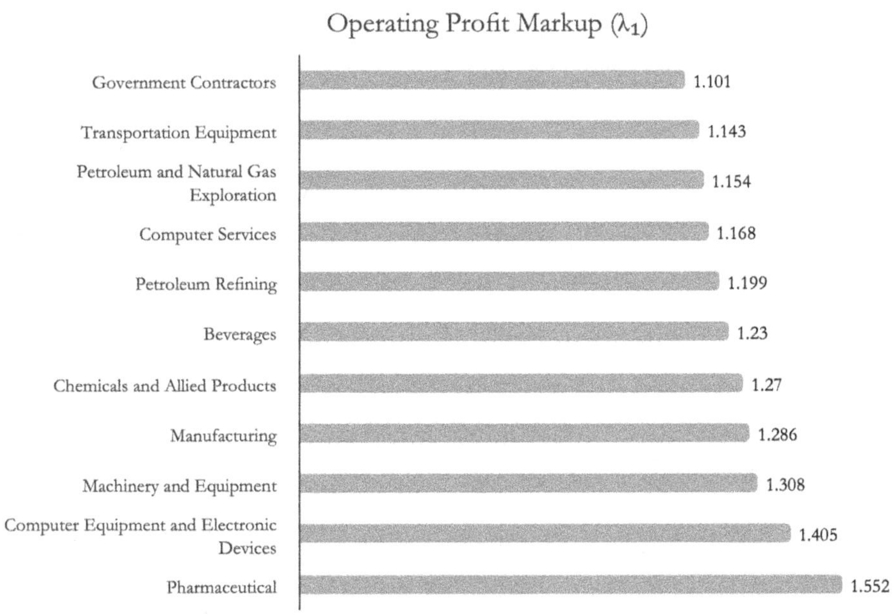

Exhibit 14.1 Industry markup

[1]Abstract from the intercept and let REVT = λ_1 XOPR, which is my equation (1.1). For a constant slope coefficient for the period examined, a change in XOPR leads to a proportional change in REVT. Thus, ΔREVT = λ_1 ΔXOPR, in which the causal direction goes from ΔXOPR to ΔREVT, mediated by the slope coefficient. Except in a few oligopolies such as computers and related devices, cost-reducing technical innovations, including robotization, have not produced decreased REVT per unit product (unit price). In the pharmaceutical industry, the increased drug and medical devices prices are scandalous—where the operating profit markup stability shown here likely reflects accounting subterfuges, such as discretionary impairment hidden in deductible COGS or XSGA, and advertising.

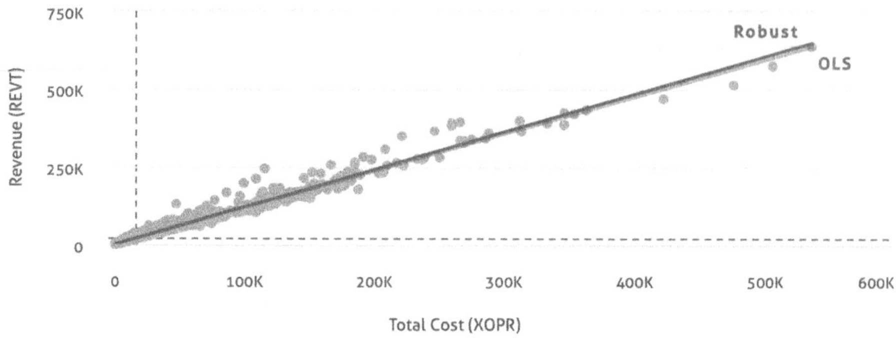

Exhibit 14.2 All companies (Count: 4337)

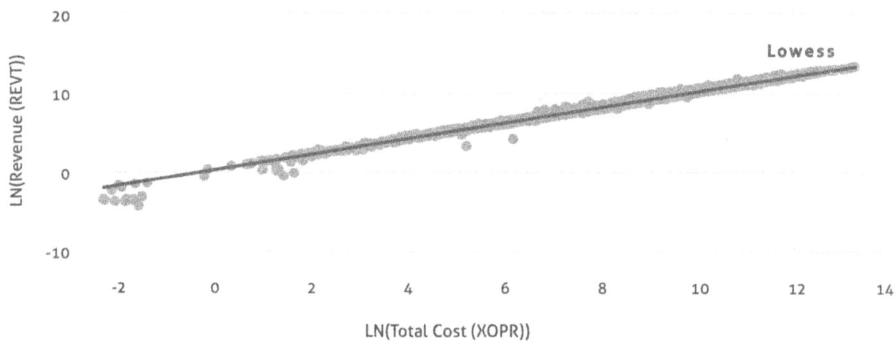

Exhibit 14.3 All companies (LN) (Count: 4337)

Exhibit 14.4 Regression summary: all industries 1950–2024 ($REVT = \lambda_0 + \lambda_1\ XOPR + \lambda_2\ PPI$)

Industry	Year range	Count	λ_0	λ_1	t-Stat	$\underline{R}^2$
Petroleum and natural gas	1950–2024	328	Y	1.15	74.5	0.988
Beverages	1950–2024	222	Y	1.23	57.3	0.995
Manufacturing	1950–2024	386	N	1.29	29.5	0.986
Pharmaceutical preparations	1950–2024	514	N	1.55	49.2	0.989
Chemicals and allied products	1950–2024	417	Y	1.27	43.0	0.993
Petroleum refining	1950–2024	351	N	1.196	113.7	0.996
Machinery and equipment	1950–2024	270	N	1.31	53.2	0.996
Computer equipment and electronic devices	1950–2024	375	N	1.41	30.9	0.980
Transportation equipment	1950–2024	551	N	1.14	91.4	0.997
Government contractors	1950–2024	566	Y	1.10	63.3	0.995
Computer services	1950–2024	357	Y	1.17	22.4	0.973
All industries	*1950–2024*	*4337*	*Y*	*1.20*	*58.9*	*0.982*

Appendix 1: Derivation of the Profit Markup Equation

I employ a straightforward regression model that is easy to follow. First, define the individual company variables: total cost (XOPR), revenue (REVT), and operating profit before depreciation and amortization (OIBDP). Total cost is the sum of the GAAP or IFRS accounts cost of goods sold (COGS) and operating expenses (XSGA).

I examine both an accounting profit (identity) equation and a structural (behavior) profit equation:

$$REVT = XOPR + OIBDP \tag{1a}$$

which is the corporation-level accounting equation (true by definition).

$$OIBDP = \beta\, REVT + \alpha \tag{2a}$$

is a linear (behavioral) profit equation (for $0 < \beta < 1$).[1]

Substitute the structural Eq. (2a) into the accounting identity (1a) and obtain the reduced-form equation used to estimate the operating profit markup:[2]

$$REVT = \lambda_0 + \lambda_1\, XOPR \tag{3a}$$

The coefficients of Eq. (3a) consist of the intercept and slope coefficients:

$$\lambda_0 = \alpha / (1 - \beta) \tag{4a}$$

is the intercept.

[1] I abstract from the residual error in structural Eq. (2a) and the reduced-form Eq. (3a) to simplify the algebra.

[2] Equation (3a) can also be derived from the Amoroso or Lerner Condition. See Amoroso (1930) and Lerner (1934).

E. A. Silva, *U.S. Corporate Profits, 1950–2024*, SpringerBriefs in Economics, https://doi.org/10.1007/978-3-032-11399-3

$$\lambda_1 = 1/(1-\beta) = 1 + \beta + \beta^2 + \beta^3 + \ldots \tag{5a}$$

is the slope coefficient.

I can derive the operating profit margin from the markup coefficient. The indirect least squares (ILS) coefficient for structural Eq. (2a) indicates the profit margin.

$$\beta = (\lambda_1 - 1)/\lambda_1 \tag{6a}$$

To my knowledge, no other author has specified the corporate or aggregate (economy-wide) operating profits markup as a two-equation system from which a reduced-form equation is selected for econometric estimation.

A significant intercept indicates that the quartiles of the univariate profit margin ratio are invalid due to the relationship between profit margin and net sales. Equation (5a) represents the operating profit markup, from which the operating profit margin is derived using indirect least squares (ILS).

Since linear Eq. (2a) is a proposed hypothesis, other functional forms, such as power functions, can be evaluated to determine the most reliable measure of the regression coefficients. In this book, I show that a simple linear reduced-form equation (1.2) produces good statistical fit, except in the case noted in this book in which a power function (double logarithms) provides more reliable estimates of the operating profit markup.

Appendix 2: Producer Price Index: All Commodities (PPIACO) (1982 = 100), Annual, from January 1950 through May 2025

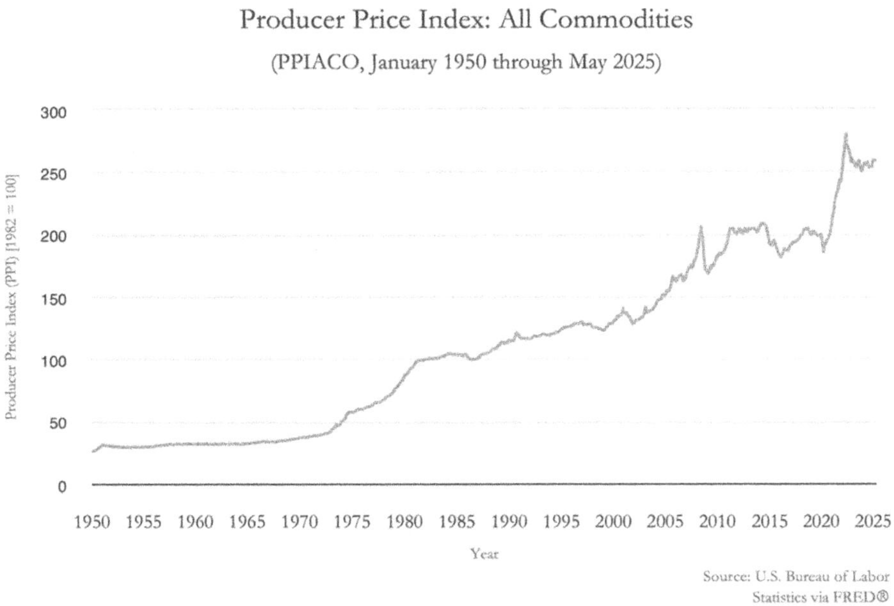

E. A. Silva, *U.S. Corporate Profits, 1950–2024*, SpringerBriefs in Economics,
https://doi.org/10.1007/978-3-032-11399-3

Appendix 3: US Manufacturing Employment (MANEMP) as a Share of Civilian Employment (CE16OV), Monthly, Seasonally Adjusted, from January 1950 Through May 2025

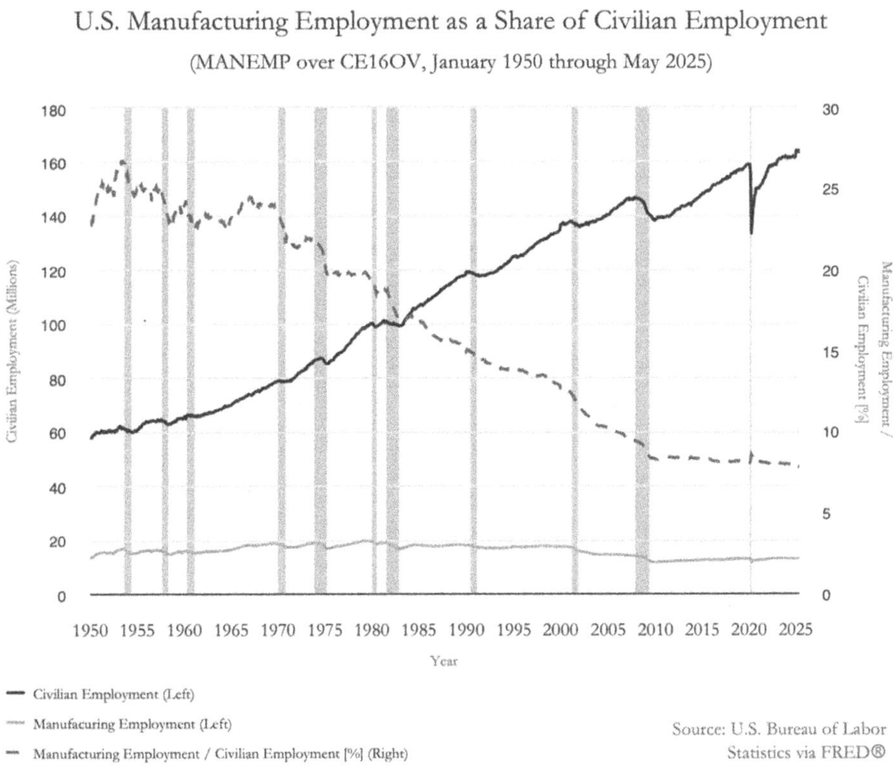

E. A. Silva, *U.S. Corporate Profits, 1950–2024*, SpringerBriefs in Economics,
https://doi.org/10.1007/978-3-032-11399-3

Appendix 4: Distribution of Operating Profit Markups Among Major US Corporations

This appendix summarizes the cross-sectional distribution of operating profit markups, estimated as the slope coefficient of XOPR in the corporation-level regression equation:

$$REVT = \lambda_0 + \lambda_1 XOPR + \lambda_2 PPI.$$

The raw data are written on Exhibit 2. The histogram (the primary statistical tool employed by Stigler (1963)) below shows the relative frequency of the 72 operating profit markups with a Burr XII (Singh-Maddala) curve overlaid.[1] Two QQ plots against the normal and lognormal distributions demonstrate systematic deviations from the reference or diagonal line.

The QQ plot of the Singh-Maddala distribution shows a better fit (less deviations from the diagonal or reference line). The Burr XII algorithm fits better the asymmetric data distribution, containing low and high outliers, and tail thickness.

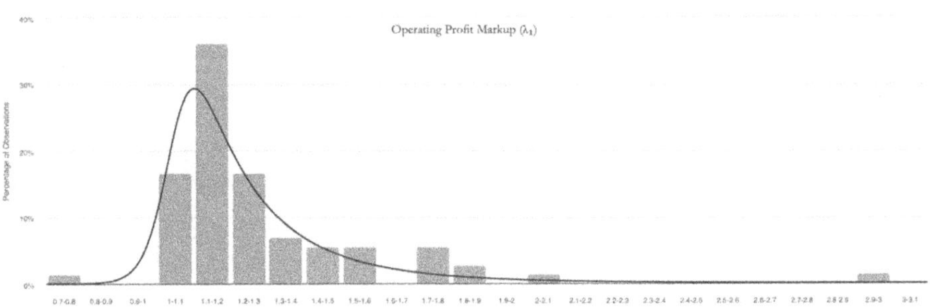

Exhibit 1 Histogram

[1] Details about the normal, lognormal, and Burr XII (Singh-Maddala) statistical distributions are found in Kleiber and Kotz (2003). The Singh-Maddala distribution is discussed in Sect. 6.2.

E. A. Silva, *U.S. Corporate Profits, 1950–2024*, SpringerBriefs in Economics,
https://doi.org/10.1007/978-3-032-11399-3

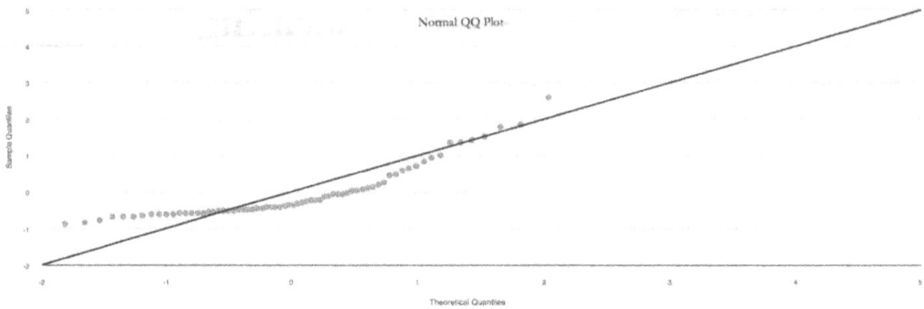

Exhibit 2 Normal distribution

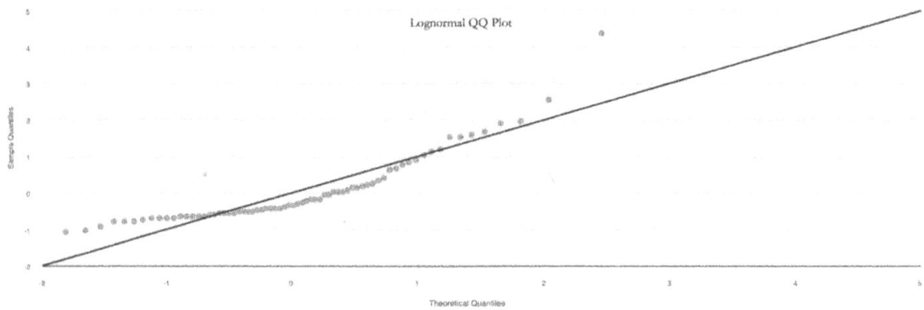

Exhibit 3 Lognormal distribution

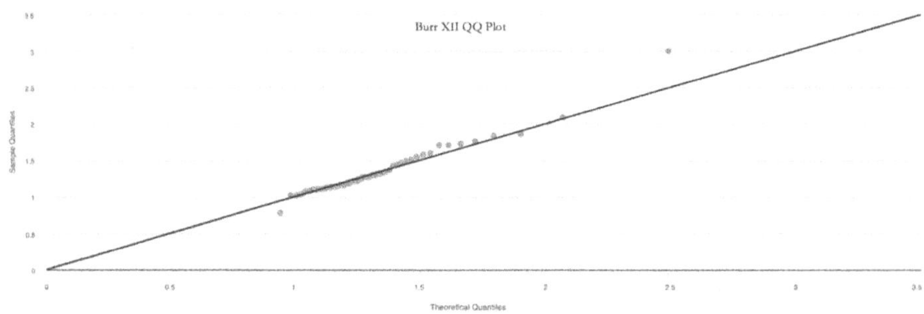

Exhibit 4 Burr XII distribution

Appendix 5: Major Products and Recent Developments Such as Acquisitions, Divestitures, and Spin-Offs

Companies	GVKEY	Main products
3M	7435	Abrasives, adhesives, advanced materials, automotive parts and hardware, building materials, cleaning supplies, coatings, compounds and polishes, dental and orthodontics, electrical materials, electronics materials and components, films and sheeting, filtration and separation, home goods, insulation, lab supplies and testing, labels, lubricants, medical supplies, office supplies, personal protective equipment, signage and marking, tapes, tools and equipment
Abbott	1078	Cardiovascular devices, continuous glucose monitors, diagnostics equipment, infant nutrition, medical nutrition, neuromodulation systems
Adobe	12540	Acrobat Pro, after effects, animate, audition, bridge, character animator, creative cloud, Dreamweaver, illustrator, InDesign, Lightroom, media encoder, Photoshop, premiere pro, substance 3D, XD
Aerojet Rocketdyne	5018	Advanced electric propulsion system, engines for expendable and reusable launch vehicles, maneuvering propulsion systems, monopropellant and bipropellant chemical thrusters, Next Generation Interceptor (NGI), propulsion, nuclear propulsion systems, RL10 engine, scramjets, solid rocket boosters, solid rocket motor boosters for hypersonic missiles, space shuttle main engine/ space launch system engine, strategic and tactical missile motors, tactical systems and armaments, divert and attitude control system, upper-stage engines, warhead assemblies
Air products & chemicals	1209	Atmospheric gases (oxygen, nitrogen, hydrogen, helium, argon), equipment and technologies (equipment for gas distribution, liquefied natural gas (LNG) technologies), performance materials (specialty surfactants and amines, polyurethane, epoxy curatives and resins, advanced coatings and adhesives), specialty gases (rare gases, carbon dioxide, carbon monoxide, syngas)

(continued)

E. A. Silva, *U.S. Corporate Profits, 1950–2024*, SpringerBriefs in Economics,
https://doi.org/10.1007/978-3-032-11399-3

Companies	GVKEY	Main products
Alphabet	160329	Android operating system, Google calendar, calico, deep mind, Fitbit, Gmail, Google chrome, Google fiber, Google maps, Google Nest home products, Google pixel smartphones, Google play store, Google search smart watches, verily, Waymo, wing, X (formerly Google X), YouTube
Amazon	64768	Alexa, Amazon prime services, Amazon web Services (AWS), Echo smart speakers, fire tablets, fire TV, kindle, retail goods
AMD	1161	Accelerated processing units (APUs), embedded processors, graphics cards (Radeon), microprocessors (Ryzen, EPYC, Threadripper), semi-custom chips
American motors	1517	Automobiles, automotive parts (historical), engines, jeeps, off-road vehicles
Apple	1690	AirPods, Apple Music, Apple TV+, Apple Watch, iCloud, iMac, iPad, iPhone, MacBook, Mac Pro, Software (macOS, iOS), Subscriptions (Apple One)
Applied Materials	1704	Applied global services (AGS), artificial intelligence (AI), internet of Things (IoT), automotive data centers, display and adjacent markets, energy-efficient glass, flexible electronics and packaging, industrial applications, medical technology and pharmaceuticals, semiconductor products, solar photovoltaics (PV)
Ashland	1794	Additives for architectural and industrial coatings, wetting agents, defoamers, and adhesion promoters, additives for cement, gypsum, mortars, and compounds, additives for oilfield applications, pressure-sensitive adhesives, structural adhesives, and laminating adhesives, controlled release polymers, disintegrants, tablet coatings, binders, excipients for both oral and injectable medications, functional molecules, and additives, ingredients for hair, oral care products, ingredients for skin, stabilizers, emulsifiers, and thickeners
Avery Dennison	1913	Apparel solutions, digital ink solutions, graphics solutions, identification solutions, label and packaging materials, medical products, performance polymers, performance tapes and adhesives
Baxter	2086	Advanced surgical equipment and digital health solutions, dialysis therapies, including products for both peritoneal dialysis (PD) and hemodialysis (HD), hemostats and sealants, hospital products, infusion systems and devices, inhaled anesthetics, parenteral nutrition (PN) therapies, remote patient management platforms, specialty injectable pharmaceuticals
Boeing	2285	Advanced information and communication systems, advanced technology solutions, commercial airplanes, commercial aviation services, defense, space, and security systems, launch systems including the Delta rocket family and the sea launch commercial launch services, performance-based logistics, satellites

(continued)

Companies	GVKEY	Main products
Bristol-Myers	2403	Abecma (idecabtagene vicleucel), a cell therapy for blood cancers; Breyanzi (lisocabtagene maraleucel), a cell therapy for blood cancers; Camzyos (mavacamten), a treatment for hypertrophic cardiomyopathy; Eliquis (apixaban), a blood thinner for preventing blood clots; Opdivo (nivolumab), a cancer therapy; Orencia (abatacept), a drug used in the treatment of rheumatoid arthritis; Revlimid (lenalidomide), a drug for blood cancers; Sotyktu (deucravacitinib), a treatment for plaque psoriasis; Yervoy (ipilimumab), an immunotherapy for cancer
Brown-Forman	2435	Ready-to-drink (new mix, Korbel), tequila (el Jimador, Herradura), whiskey and American whiskey (Jack Daniel's, old forester, Slane, Woodford reserve)
Caterpillar	2817	Articulated trucks, backhoe loaders, dozers, engines, excavators, generators, motor graders, skid steer loaders, wheel loaders, parts and fluids
Celanese	162,254	Acetyl emulsions and powders (for coatings and adhesives), advanced engineered plastics (acetal polymers, liquid crystal polymers, UHMW polyethylene), chemical intermediates for pharmaceuticals, films, inks, polymers for consumer goods, resin, solvents
Chevron	2991	Aviation gasoline, diesel fuel, jet fuel, lubricants and engine oils (e.g., Havoline®, Delo®), motor gasoline, petrochemicals, ship fuels and marine oils
Cisco	20,779	Access networking switches, data-center networking, industrial IoT networking, network security and software, optical networking, routers, wireless APs, silicon and interface modules
Clark equipment	3091	Forklifts order pickers, pallet stackers, pallet trucks, tugger trains, bobcat equipment, Daken farm equipment, Develon, Doosan portable power, FINN equipment, grasshopper mowers, Mantsinen, McCormick, tractors, omega heavy trucks, Terberg, tow tractors
Coca-Cola	3144	Carbonated soft drinks (e.g., Coca-Cola, sprite, Fanta), coffee and tea RTD, dairy and plant-based drinks, juice drinks, sports drinks, water and flavored water
ConocoPhillips	8549	Bitumen, crude oil, LNG, natural gas, natural gas liquids, oil and gas exploration, petrochemical feedstocks
Cummins	3650	Alternative fuel, diesel and gas engines, power systems and generators, components (filtration, turbochargers, fuel systems, emission solutions, electronics), marine engines
Curtiss-Wright	3662	Aerospace, defense actuators, and valves; aircraft sensors and controls; EMS division pumps, steam turbines, electrical and mechanical systems; industrial sensors and HMIs; subsystems for naval and nuclear power
CVR energy	178,672	Petroleum refining, fuels (gasoline, diesel), renewable diesel, renewable fuel production (biofuels), petroleum storage and logistics (not extensive public breakdown available)

(continued)

Companies	GVKEY	Main products
Dana	3734	Automotive axles, driveshafts, transmissions, sealing products, thermal and drive technologies, lightweight vehicle power train systems
Deere & co.	3835	Attachments for tractors, crop care, drivetrain components, earthmoving equipment, engines, forestry equipment, frontier™ equipment for property maintenance, gator™ utility vehicles, harvesters, hay and forage, mowers, tractors
Dupont de Nemours	4060	Adhesives, advanced materials, biomaterials, clean technology solutions, construction materials (e.g., Tyvek®), consumer products (e.g., Corian®), electronics materials, fabrics and fibers (e.g., Kevlar®, Nomex®), healthcare solutions, industrial films
DXC technology	3336	Cybersecurity services, DXC cloud, DXC insurance software, DXC modern workplace, DXC platform X™.
EDS	5074	Business process outsourcing (BPO), information technology services (IT), product life cycle management, systems integration
Eli Lilly	6730	Diabetes and obesity treatments (e.g., Mounjaro, Zepbound), oncology drugs (e.g., Verzenio), psychiatric and mental health medications, widely used insulin products
Exxon	4503	Chemicals, crude oil, energy products, lubricants, marine fuels, Mobil 1 (synthetic motor oil), petrochemicals, renewable/ low-emission technologies
Ford motor	4839	Electric vehicles, hybrid vehicles, internal combustion vehicles (cars, SUVs, trucks), vehicle parts and services (e.g., Motorcraft brand)
General Dynamics	5046	Business jets (e.g., gulfstream), command and control systems, combat vehicles (e.g., Abrams tanks, Stryker, Ajax), military ships and submarines, secure communications and intelligence systems
General motors	5073	Automobiles (Chevrolet, Buick, GMC, Cadillac), commercial vehicles, electric vehicles, internal combustion vehicles, military platforms (via GM defense), vehicle parts and services
Goodyear tire & rubber	5234	Bicycle, aviation, commercial truck, motorcycle, off-road machinery, passenger vehicle, performance racing, tires
Hess	1380	Crude oil, natural gas, petrochemicals, propane
HF Sinclair	5667	Asphalt, diesel fuel, gasoline, jet fuel, lubricants and specialty fluids, renewable diesel, specialty chemicals and modified asphalt
Honeywell international	1300	Aerospace (aircraft engines, avionics, auxiliary power units, sensors), building automation systems, filters and purifiers, industrial automation and control products, safety and productivity solutions (e.g., barcode scanners, mobile computers, protective equipment), specialty chemicals and materials
HP	5606	3D printers, desktops, laptops, monitors, personal computers (consumer and business), printers (e.g., DeskJet, LaserJet, OfficeJet, envy), scanners
Huntsman	162,401	Adhesives, amines, advanced materials and composites, maleic anhydride, polyurethanes (MDI systems), surfactants and performance chemicals

(continued)

Companies	GVKEY	Main products
IBM	6066	Cloud and AI software platforms (e.g., watsonx), consulting and digital transformation services, hybrid cloud infrastructure, hardware (mainframes, quantum systems, power microprocessors)
Intel	6008	CPUs (e.g., Core, Xeon, atom), field-programmable gate arrays (FPGAs), graphics cards (e.g., arc), memory and storage devices, network interface controllers and wireless products
Johnson & Johnson	6266	Medical devices (e.g., surgical staplers, tissue repair systems), orthopedics and vision technologies, oncology, immunology, neuroscience, cardiopulmonary therapies
Kimberly-Clark Corp	6435	Baby and child care (e.g., Huggies), feminine hygiene (e.g., Kotex), incontinence products (e.g., depend), tissues and wipes (e.g., Kleenex, Cottonelle), toilet paper and paper towels (e.g., Scott, viva)
L3Harris	5492	Avionics and electronic systems, C3ISR (command, control, communications, intelligence, surveillance, recon), antennas (terrestrial and spaceborne), RF and telemetry systems, tactical radios, training and simulation systems
Lockheed Martin	6774	Aircraft (F35, C130, F16, helicopters), ballistic missiles (trident II), cybersecurity and command systems (aegis combat system), missiles and fire control (JASSM, patriot, LRASM), space systems (Orion, GPS, hypersonic weapons)
Marathon oil	7017	Crude oil and natural gas production (US unconventional)
Marathon petroleum	186,989	Lubricants and motor oils, petrochemicals (e.g., propylene, benzene), specialty products (e.g., asphalt, anode, and fuel-grade coke)
Merck	7257	Biologic therapies, companion animal health products, key prescription medicines (e.g., Januvia, Keytruda), vaccines (e.g., Gardasil, ProQuad), hospital acute-care drugs
Microsoft	12,141	AI tools (copilot), azure cloud services, gaming consoles and services (e.g., Xbox), office suite (Microsoft 365), operating systems (e.g., windows), productivity apps (e.g., teams, word, excel), surface devices
Mosaic	162,129	Phosphate fertilizers, potash fertilizers
Murphy oil	7620	Crude oil, natural gas
Navistar international	6081	Commercial trucks, diesel engines, school and commercial buses (IC bus), vocational vehicles, vehicle service parts, financing solutions (for fleets)
Northrop	7985	Autonomous systems, B-21 raider and B-2 Spirit stealth bombers, battle management and command systems, global hawk (unmanned surveillance aircraft), James Webb space telescope (JWST), missile interceptors and defense systems, spacecraft and launch systems, synthetic crystals and optical components, propulsion systems (bipropellant, monopropellant, gel)
Nvidia	117,768	Automotive platforms (e.g., DRIVE), compute and networking hardware, data-center GPUs and systems (DGX, HGX, Blackwell architecture), graphics GPUs (GeForce, RTX), networking DPUs (BlueField), support tools and software (CUDA, Maxine, Omniverse)

(continued)

Companies	GVKEY	Main products
Occidental petroleum	8068	Basic chemicals and vinyls, crude oil and condensate, midstream and marketing of oil, natural gas liquids, natural gas, natural gas liquids
Oracle	12,142	Cloud infrastructure and applications (e.g., OCI, AI, autonomous database), engineered hardware systems (Exadata, servers, storage), enterprise applications (e.g., E-business suite, PeopleSoft), middleware and developer tools (Java, Linux)
Owens corning	8214	Asphalt roofing shingles, building insulation (fiberglass), composite materials, fiberglass rebar and reinforcements
Par Pacific holdings	22,447	Biofuels, diesel fuel (ultralow sulfur), gasoline (unleaded clear, E10), jet fuel, prepared food and sundries at fuel retail outlets
PepsiCo	8479	Beverages (e.g., Gatorade, Pepsi-cola, mountain dew, Rockstar energy, soda), cereals and oats, convenient snack foods (e.g., lay's, Doritos, Quaker), ready-to-drink coffees
Pfizer	8530	Biopharmaceutical drugs (e.g., Eliquis, Ibrance, Prevnar, Vyndaqel), vaccines (e.g., Comirnaty, RSV vaccine ABRYSVO™, ABRILADA™), COVID-19 antivirals (e.g., Paxlovid)
PPG industries	8247	Coatings and paints (architectural, industrial, automotive, marine, protective), decorative paints, sealants and adhesives, specialty materials
Procter & gamble	8762	Baby care (e.g., pampers), fabric and home care products (e.g., tide, Mr. clean), feminine care (always), grooming (Gillette, Braun), hair, skin and personal care, oral and personal healthcare products
RTX	10,983	Aerostructures, aircraft engines (commercial and military), auxiliary power units, avionics, cabin interiors, communication systems, landing gear, missile defense, precision weapons, radar
Textron	10,519	Aircraft (e.g., Beechcraft, Cessna), armored vehicles, bell helicopters, drones, golf carts, industrial tools, marine systems
Trecora resources	1712	Custom processing services, high-purity hydrocarbons, specialty petrochemicals, waxes
Unisys	2504	Cloud management services, cybersecurity software, digital workplace solutions, enterprise computing systems, mainframe services
Valero energy	15,247	Diesel fuel, ethanol, gasoline, jet fuel, petrochemical feedstocks
Xilinx	22,325	Adaptive SoCs, FPGAs, high-speed data converters, semiconductor IP, software design tools

Bibliography

Amoroso L (1930) La Curva Statica Di Offerta. Giornale Degli Economisti e Rivista Di Statistica 70 (Anno 45)(1):1–26. http://www.jstor.org/stable/23227293

Bain J (1956) Barriers to new competition. Harvard University Press

Chandler A (1962) Strategy and structure: chapters in the history of industrial enterprise. MIT Press

Congressional Budget Office (2020, September) An update to the budget outlook: 2020 to 2030 (Publication No. 57126). https://www.cbo.gov/publication/57126

Gschwandtner A (2012) Evolution of profit persistence in the USA: evidence from three periods. Manch Sch 80(2)

Kalecki M (1965) Theory of economic dynamics, 2nd edn. George Allen & Unwin

Kleiber C, Kotz S (2003) Statistical size distributions in economics and actuarial sciences. Wiley

Kmenta J (1986) Elements of econometrics, 2nd edn. Macmillan

Lerner A (1934) The concept of monopoly and the measurement of monopoly power. Rev Econ Stud 1(3):157–175. https://doi.org/10.2307/2967480

Modigliani F (1958) New developments on the oligopoly front. J Polit Econ 66(3):215–232. http://www.jstor.org/stable/1833215

Mueller D (1986) Profits in the long run. Cambridge University Press

Mueller D (ed) (1990) The dynamics of company profits (An international comparison). Cambridge University Press

Stigler G (1963) Capital and rates of return in manufacturing industries. Princeton University Press

Sylos-Labini P (1969) Oligopoly and technical progress. Harvard University Press

E. A. Silva, *U.S. Corporate Profits, 1950–2024*, SpringerBriefs in Economics,
https://doi.org/10.1007/978-3-032-11399-3

www.ingramcontent.com/pod-product-compliance
Lightning Source LLC
Chambersburg PA
CBHW060249200126
38433CB00012B/496
9783032113986